WHERE SONGS DO THUNDER

WHERE SONGS DO THUNDER

Travels in Traditional Song

Paddy Tunney

APPLETREE PRESS

*To the troubadours of Ireland
who kept our songs as
live as running water.*

First published and printed by
The Appletree Press Ltd
7 James Street South
Belfast BT2 8DL
1991

This book has received support from
the Cultural Traditions Programme
of the Community Relations Council,
which aims to encourage acceptance
and understanding of cultural diversity.

British Library Cataloguing-in-Publication Data
A catalogue record for this book is
available from the British Library.

Typeset by Falcon Typographic Art Ltd,
Edinburgh & London

ISBN 0 86281 292 5

9 8 7 6 5 4 3 2 1

Contents

1

The Blackberry Blossom

It was Lammas Fair time and the weather had not broken. Meadows were fragrant with clover and coltsfoot and, where bramble bristled through high hedgerows, blackberry blossom flourished in wild profusion. The turf in the bog was bone dry and had shrunk to the size of scythe whetstones. It would have to be gathered and drawn home at once.

My brother Joe was the first to leave the street, with McGlinchey's big cut-jack yoked to the cart Owen Doherty put together for us. His destination was the turf bank on Harte's Hill for a load of black clods to fuel the fire in the room grate. Yankees were due any day now and they were always a cold-rife crew winter or summer.

I waited until he passed Derryhallow School on the New Line Road and then threw the greth and creels on our own ass and set out for Cruckacarry bog to drag out brown turf.

Joe and I swapped tunes down the valley between John Ned's bridge and Cox's Causeway, but the bulk of Larkhill put an end to the musical exchange and it wasn't until I reached Lawn's Level that I was able to make contact with him again. On the top of Hughie's John's hill I came face to face with Pat Meehan, weighed down with a long clarendo bag of turf. As soon as he saw me, he made a beeline for the resting place in the sod fence and sat down beneath his load. I was still lilting away as I approached him.

'What was that reel you were lilting?' the little man asked.

'*The Blackberry Blossom*', I said.

'Wrong!' he admonished. 'Smart a boy as you think you are, in old God's time we called that tune *The Newbridge Fair*.'

It was a bright, clear evening. The sun was spilling gold into the narrow gorge of the Scardan River and lark song got lost in the high blue dome of the sky. Across the heathery breeze that rippled through ripening corn came the clearest, truest whistling we were ever likely to hear again. Meehan spragged the bag of turf on the ditch with a clod and leaped out on to the centre of the road.

'Wheesht!' he commanded. 'Ah! That's *The Blackberry Blossom*! By damn, but it must be the "wee people" that's in it! Would it be unlucky to dance to their music, do you think?'

'Dance away', I assured him. 'That's not "gentle" music.'

And then we saw him as beast and vehicle topped the *ailts* on the New Line Road. He was standing up in the cart and as he came into full view it was plain he was flaking out reel steps on the bed of the vehicle between the wing-boards.

'Almighty God!' shouted Meehan, now wildly excited. 'Did you ever hear the likes of that whistling! It's not earthly. The time and the lift of it! By God, you could walk on music like that.' Then he began to dance.

'Face me there, Paddy. It's a poor thing to be dancin' alone.'

I jumped on to the road and went through the motions just to please him, for I never was a great hand with the feet. I chose a level, smooth spot where the Lammas floods had left a light skintling of sand. I wasn't going to risk getting a stone bruise or a skinned heel, for I was putting God's leather to God's weather at the time and only wore shoes on Sunday.

Meehan was safe enough. He wore a heavy pair of pavers and so could crig and clatter on a flat flag and send splanks flying in all directions in true traditional manner. He was a dapper little man, as straight as a yard of pumped water, and

wore a sweeping brown moustache a couple of sizes too big
for him.

Oh, for those days of youth and love and laughter when
hearts were light and steps were free! I sometimes wonder if
those two splendid reel dancers haven't worn away the flags
of heaven's floor, for the merry do love to dance.

The ass made it to the hollow below the brae where rain
had washed down a scattering of fine sand. Here she halted
and began pawing the sand.

'Away like the hammers of hell', shouted Meehan. 'She's
about to lie down and walter.'

I hurried down the hill, but before I could get her length
she threw herself down, wriggled free of creels and greth and
began waltering in the sand. Rolling over twice, she jumped
up, shook herself free of sand, hee-hawed mournfully and
bolted for home. I grabbed the trailing reins as she bounded
past. Straining, I put a sudden stop to her gallop, jumped on
her back and rode her hell for leather down the brae again.
The belly-band and crupper were in flitters. One peg of the
straddle-crutch was undone. One of the creels was lying on
its mouth and nose in a *sheugh* of spa water. In those days
boys never ventured forth to push their fortunes without a
pocketfull of Hairy Ned string, and so I was able to repair
the damage done and dragged out turf until the stars were
on the sky.

When blackberry blossoms berried and ripened as black
and shiny as sloe, there was a song to honour their maturing.
It's called *Na Smeara*, or *The Blackberries*, and was composed
in the native tongue by J P Craig, a teacher in Saint Eunan's
College, Letterkenny, round about the early decades of this
century. It was taught to me by Hudie Devanney, that fine
traditional singer from Rannefast, in the winter of 1948:

THE BLACKBERRIES
In the airy, merry harvest time, and I footloose and
    fancy-free

With a wish for every woman, and I herding horny cows
I met a dark-eyed damsel, and she plucking ripened
    blackberries
I fell head and heels in love with her among the nutting
    boughs.
From sunrise to evening star 'twas I who was the
    Romeo
A'wooing of this bonnie lass who swiped my heart
    away
And left me in the latter end all moidered, without
    house or home
And I so keen to be her mate until my dying day.

Chorus:
I keep thinking of the berries and the wild birds of the
    air
I keep thinking of my sweetheart and her features fine
    and fair
When she pledged faith and fidelity, I loved her more
    and more
And we among the blackberries at heart of harvest's
    core.

At the shearing, sheafing, stooking time, my soul was
    all serenity
The maidens of the parish all with them I was in love
I flirted with them far and near: they winked and
    nodded knowingly
They swore I was their glamour boy; a blessing from
    above.
At last I knelt and worshipped at the shrine of Peg
    O'Doherty
The tidings of engagement they were in the press next
    day
But heavens! One day later, boys, as true as thrush is
    warbling
She vanished with a vagabond; a soldier boy, they say.

Chorus

One day says I for devilment to the widow from the
    Yellow Crag
'Tis you who are unfortunate with benweed on your
    land
When you should be close-spancelled to a *spalpeen*, stall
    or lusty stag
If you're looking for a candidate, I tell you now I'll
    stand.'
In standing leaps she left my sight and ram-stammed up
    the kitchen floor
A 'car' on her face that would frighten friend and foe
It wasn't long till back she came with boiling water in
    a can
And boys! she nearly scalded me, my black and bitter
    woe!

Donkeys may be stupid animals, but they are wild, stubborn and contrary too. I mind well an ass we had one
time, a cut-jack it was, that totally rejected the humdrum
life of a eunuch. Instead, he took to rambling like some
haughty, high-stepping stallion and teased and tantalised
all the dainty little mare donkeys in the area when they were
in heat. To curb his vagrant tendencies to some extent, my
brother Michael fixed a cow chain round his neck to which
was fastened a five-foot long holly wattle. The swivel on the
chain assured that Romeo wouldn't hang himself if he got
into a tight corner or stuck his wattle in thick undergrowth.
For some time it did inhibit his inclination to clear high
fences, but in time he devised a method whereby he overcame
his handicap. He manoeuvred the wattle to the left side of his
neck. Then, by a deft throw backwards of the head, he swung
the holly stick on to his broad shoulders and balanced it there.
    For all the world he looked like one of Sean McHugh's five
and forty Hearts of Oak, who came from the shores of Lough

Erne, going off to a faction fight with his cudgel over his
shoulder. Jimmie Lannigan lived two townlands away. He
was the proud owner of a lovely little mare donkey which,
they said, was fleeter than the wind. He was feeding her on
oats and getting her into good condition for the donkey
derby in Clabby come the fifteenth of August. However,
as my very good friend Sean O'Gallchobhair from Derry
would say, nature defies convention. So the maiden mare
beyond compare sent out signals that mating with her was
a must.

Romeo was out on the rocks among the blooming heather
and was first to hear her heated hee-hawing as it reached
him down a south-west wind, mingled with the fragrance
of woodbine and wild roses. Passion stirred in the blood
of the noble beast despite the terrible wrong inflicted upon
him by a heartless ass gelder. He gave a snore and a snort,
threw the wattle over his shoulder and cleared the high
stone ditch at the road like a thoroughbred going over
beechers. Sean McArt, on his way to court in Upper Scardan,
met him going up the Miller's brae on his hind legs, his
tail out and his mouth open. He duly relayed the information to my brother Michael. Fine well we knew his
destination.

I must say Michael didn't let the tidings interfere with
his sleep.

'Let the hare sit until morning', he said. 'Then Paddy here
can go and bail him out. Jimmie hasn't been speaking to you
since you came home and so he's unlikely to chew the rag too
much with you. Anyhow, you can handle the likes of them
buckoes better. I'd only get thick and get him by the throat
and maybe have to give him a couple of hard boxes. Sure a
man wouldn't know how to hit him and at the same time
save his life!'

Around dinner-time the following day I headed for Lan-
nigans. Peter Moohan, whom I met on the *cruckin*, informed
me that Romeo was 'in the pound' and that Jimmie was not
in the best of twist. 'Take him canny', he counselled, 'and

whatever you say, say nothing.' A wink was as good as a nod, and indeed I was thankful for the forewarning.

Going up the street I was greeted by a fine flock of turkeys, already nearly full grown. So great was their welcome that I got it tight to make my way to the half-door. They gobbled and strutted, dropped purple chullers and fanned out tail feathers.

Jimmie beckoned me inside without saying a word. By the sneds of him, it was patently plain he was not in the best of good humour. I seized the initiative. 'Well, Jimmie!' I saluted him. 'Damn it, that's the finest flock of turkeys I've seen for a very long time.' It worked. Reluctantly he fell for the flattery.

'Here and be God! They're good turkeys, right enough, Patrick', he growled, somewhat mollified, 'But wouldn't it be a bugger if the cocks were too heavy come the turkey market?'

He advanced and held out a grimy, calloused paw. 'You're welcome, anyhow', he went on and gave me a firm hand-shake. He had been washing grey twill shirts in a sawed-off tar barrel that stood in the centre of the kitchen floor and, it goes without saying, the garments came out much blacker than they went in. Still, there was that fine, pungent smell of tar off them and I had no doubt that although they were black, they were well disinfected. It's hard to whack the tar. Steam rose from the tar barrel. The fire of wet green logs and half-dry rough-heads hissed and spluttered morosely, and the smoke from the blow-down in the chimney would have reddened the eyes of an Australian aborigine.

When the wind changed and the draught in the chimney improved a little, I made out the form of a mighty man lying away back in a chair beside the hearth, puffing contentedly at his pipe. It was Big Thomas the Canadian, once the prize fighter of the entire parish. Even now he still carried the belt, and a couple of lesser men who got notions into their heads while he was abroad had reason to rue the day they disputed his right to do so.

A smile like fire flame on a cold, dark hearth played on his weathered features as he rose to greet me.

'Put it there if it was a tonne weight!' and he held out a hand that was as broad as the blade of a shovel.

'How do? How are you gettin' on?' There was still a trace of the Canadian drawl in the rover's speech, but his welcome was unmistakably Irish.

'I suppose you're lookin' for that ol' get of an ass of Mick's', Jimmie interjected. 'I had to close him in last night. Our wee donkey was a' jackin' and he broke down the wee stable door to get in to her. There he was pavin' away and givin' her every wallop of his big, holly wattle up the side of her jaw. I wouldn't think a hate of it if he was able to horse her, and she bein' trained for the donkey derby in Clabby come the fifteenth! What date is this? We never bother about a calendar, and for time of day we just go by the sun.'

'It's the third of August', I told him. 'Yesterday was the bank holiday.'

'That only gives us twelve days to have her ready for the race. Her left eye's shut and she has a couple of cuts on her hind-quarters he made with the caulkers of his shoes. What the hell need is it to have that buck-ass shod anyhow? Tell your brother Mick to keep his ass at home from this on. If my wee mare doesn't win the Clabby Derby, I'll hol' him responsible.'

'Arrah! Will you quit about ol' asses', Thomas admonished him. 'At least they're more sociable than the people around here. They come to see one another an odd time.'

'Alright, we'll let him go this time. Whatever time Patrick is ready to go, you give Romeo his head, Thomas. I have to clean myself up and go to Ballyshanny on a bit of business.' He washed and dressed and headed off, leading his bike by a handlebar.

I settled down in the other fireside chair, for Thomas and I had much chatting to do. The fire was now bright and blazing. Thomas stuck the black pandy in the coals and when the water was boiled he plumped a fistful of tea in it. He cut a small loaf in two, lavishly buttered both sides of the bulky slices and we fell to a tightner of strong tea, bread and butter.

'I'm sorry I haven't a better table,' he apologised, 'but since the good weather set in, the ducks stopped laying.' Then the story-telling started.

'I mind one time when I was with the British army in India', Thomas began, 'away out on the Bay of Bengal. We were on night patrol, myself and a Gurkha. Indeed, the same boyo taught me many's the trick that you couldn't learn at home from Big John Lawn or even John Mulraine, but that's another story. The terrain we were patrollin' was swampy and treacherous and we had to be very careful. To make matters worse, the night was as black as the hob of hell. The Gurkha had some oily waste about his tunic somewhere. You know, the kind of material mechanics and steam-roller men use to wipe away oil and grease. He gathered some drift-wood and tinder-dry droppings of wild birds, and then rubbed two pieces of wood together until he got a spark. It was no time till he had a cheery fire blazin' away, what with the oily waste, the drift-wood and the dried dung.

'It was then both of us took the *féar gortach*. Let no one tell you it's a disease you only get in this country. Anywhere on the face of this earth from Rathlin Island to Rangoon, or from Tara to Timbucktoo, that weakness will strike you if you walk on the hungry grass of a famine mound, and India has its share.

'We searched our haversacks. Between us we could only raise one small packet of hard biscuits, for we were on iron rations at the time. "Eureka", yelled the Gurkha. I was astounded, for I never thought the bugger had that much learnin'. "We'll use our bayonets and dig for crocodiles' eggs." The thought never struck me, I must admit, but then them Gurkhas are the devils out of hell when it comes to survival. I agreed and we crossed to a little shingle of sandy

shore that shimmered in the firelight. We started delvin',
and in the clappin' of your hands hadn't the Gurkha nine
eggs and I had three. He knew exactly where to dig. I was
only blind-stabbin'. We boiled them in an ol' billy-can with
brackish Bay of Bengal water, and to tell you the God's truth,
Paddy, no bird's egg ever tasted so sweet. 'Course they were
very fresh. I mean to say, young crocs hadn't begun to make
in them.

'Never were British bayonets put to better use since the
burial of Sir John Moore in Corunna, yon time. We ate the
dozen eggs and the biscuits, but as our water supply had
been drunk long before, we had nothing to wash the food
down with.

'It was then I spied this great crocodile wrigglin' up out
of the swamps and mud. I declare to God he must have been
sixty-feet long. He be to smell the cookin'. "Run for your
life", roared the Gurkha, and he did just that. I was hot on
his heels and we shinned up two telegraph poles just in the
nick of time. The croc came on walterin' and belly-flappin'
till he reached the pole that I had climbed. Then he started
knawin' and chawin' at the butt of the pole.

'The telegraph poles were dipped in creosote, or some
damned thing, to protect them from termites, beetles and
every devil. Besides, they were the very best Burma teak.
All this meant that my bully croc had his fill of knawin' to do
before he'd fell the pole, but he must have had the patience of
Job. He wrought away in the dark, and there was I clingin'
on the crossbar at the top, waitin' every minute to hear the
creak of splinterin' wood and the crash of the pole to the
ground. Never did I pray with such fervour, and it wasn't
to Buddha or Allah or any of them ol' buckoes I looked to
for deliverance.

'And damn it, do you know in the rear my prayers
were answered. Didn't the dawn come thunderin' up from
Chinkland side and my bold croc swivelled round and dived
into the swamp. It's likes they're not too fond of God's good
daylight. The pole was knawed almost through. It shuddered

under me and crashed down across the Burma Road. Good thing too it didn't fall into the swamp! There wouldn't have been mouthfuls a piece for the shoal of crocodiles gathered in the swampy bay, waitin' for a dawn breakfast. The place was hoachin' with them!

'Then the thirst struck us. It was bad enough durin' the night, but when the sun rose in the heavens we fair sizzled. Our throats were parched and we couldn't make spittle. When we got back to camp I could have drunk Lough Erne dry. I never had such a drought since the night myself and Big Pat Connor ate the buck goat at the still-house on the top of McCormick's hill. There was a dance and a raffle in the house youse are livin' in now. It was Pat Dram owned it then. It was the time of the Black and Tans and there was a curfew. The raffle was on the buck goat, and just as the singlin's started comin' through, didn't both of us take the *féar gortach*. We'd have damned near scobed the bark off the birches in the mearing between McCormick and Barney Deery, so great were the hunger pangs.

'Then Pat had a brain-wave. "Away to hell, Tommie, and stale the prize they're rafflin. We'll have venison of a kind for supper." I needed no second biddin'. The ol' buck came quietly and I whipped a whum out of the crate of Deery's cart on the way back to use as a roastin' spit. Three mighty bleats of mercy were all the buck gave when I drove the big barber knife home. We skinned him and cleaned him out and Pat tenderised the flesh with a douchin' of prime poteen. Man dear, when he was spit-roasted you never tasted nicer flavoured meat. The men that's goin' now couldn't eat and drink like that. If they ate more goats and drank good, wholesome poteen there would be no need for hospitals, and the doctors would have to go on the dole.

'The thirst we raised was a fearfull one indeed, but we slaked it with gallons of poteen.'

I knew every word was gospel truth, for Thomas Lannigan was never known to tell a lie, and indeed I had heard tell of

the same schism from Big Pat when I was a cub and he up
céilíng in our house.

When it was time for me to cut my stick, Thomas released
the ass and held him by the mane until I mounted. I gripped
the wattle in both hands and used it as a kind of rein. Away
we sped like a March wind and I never let him break gallop
till we landed at our house, and he in a lather of sweat.
Curious thing, he never wandered more but settled down
to the life of a sensible, civilised cut-jack.

The briar blossom blackened into berry. Nutting trees
hung heavy with hazelled health and Hallowe'en brought
its pranks and games, played out with spirit and gusto.
Girls washed shifts in south-running streams, dried them
by the hearthstone in the glow of the *greeshagh* and waited
wistfully for the faces of their future husbands to appear
in mirrors propped up with a creepy stool over by the
cricket flag as soon as the clock struck twelve. If a coffin
appeared instead, a girl would be in her grave before next
Hallowe'en. It was a daunting trick played only by reckless
damsels devoid of fear.

Young men religiously sowed their 'hard grain' on a bed-
room floor, repeating the invocation:

My hard grain I sow you
My true love, to know you
Whoever you are, appear to me this night.

They then went to bed and eagerly awaited the vision of
the *spéirbhean* with whom they would eventually wife. The
hard grain was either corn or rye, but better results were
obtained with corn. It seems that 'vision women', like their
fleshier counterparts in the material world, love to get their
corn. Rye-bread is associated with Russians, and not to be
compared with the diet of Lough Derg, which is good for the
soul and body.

Perhaps the more daring cowboys would repair to the

haggard at the murk and midnight hour and 'ride the rake' round a cornstack or two. The third time round the stack, if he was quick enough and looked round, he'd see the vision of a girl who was to become his mate for life, straddle-legged on the rake behind him. If he was to remain a bachelor, a heavy vessel of soil would be hooked on to the rake, indicating that he'd be wed to mother earth for the remainder of his natural days, toiling away from morning till night with his two ends in the ground. Such a fate could only be averted by crossing the Western ocean to America where the spell was no longer binding. Indeed, if fewer daring young men had not ridden rakes round corn stacks on Hallowe'en night, I am convinced that the exodus to the United States round the middle and late thirties would have slowed considerably, or perhaps ceased altogether.

Pat the Pagan held that in order to perform rake-riding properly, the powers of darkness, or at least those of *Crom Cruaidh*, had to be invoked. Other ancients equally wise in such matters declared that this was nonsense. The acts performed fell within the scope of white wizardry and therefore the devil should be allowed to remain in the comfort and warmth of hell on a cold Hallowe'en night without anyone putting to him or from him.

Whatever the folklore about the eve of *Samhain* and the reputed evil abroad on that night, according to Celtic tradition it was generally accepted that All Souls' Night belonged to the souls in purgatory released on one night's parole from a state of punishment and purification. On that night the fire was never raked. Instead, a great limekiln of a fire was put on at bedtime and an abundant supply of food and drink laid out near the hearth. This was meant as a sign of the loving place the departed still held in our hearts and as an assurance of our continued prayers on their behalf.

The chapel was left open until 9.00 p.m. so that the faithful could pray and make visits there for the souls of the departed friends and relatives.

It happened that Master Edmond O'Grady, school principal

and untiring worker for social and intellectual advancement, decided to call a meeting of the GAA club, the local branch of the Ulster Farmers' Union and other interested bodies to explore the possibility of building a hall or recreation centre for our corner of the parish.

It was scheduled for half past nine, a time, the convener figured, when prayers would be over and a good many souls on their way to a meeting with Peter himself at the golden gates of paradise.

We duly went along, said our prayers, made the visits and then headed for the school, where the meeting was to be held. Lanty Gorman made his visits and then repaired to his Sunday seat on the gallery, where he recited fifteen decades of the rosary. Then he fell asleep. Kate McGarrigle, the sacristan, came at the stroke of nine and, as there wasn't a sinner to be seen in the body of the building, she locked and bolted the main door.

The meeting was late in starting, for the convener did not arrive in time, and when he finally put in an appearance little heed was paid to his comment that discordant notes were issuing from the gallery of the chapel. It was plain to everyone there that the good master had had a brief but blissful meeting with a John Jameson on the way, and the same warrior was capable of playing tricks with men's ears as well as their tongues.

However, when Mick Dolan withdrew to the school yard to water the horse and returned to inform us that some person unknown was making a hames of that glorious hymn, *Faith Of Our Fathers*, it was thought that the matter must be investigated; the chairman adjourned the meeting for ten minutes and we sallied forth to identify the cause of the commotion.

'Be careful', the master cautioned us on the way. 'If it's a ghost or a spirit is uttering these notes, the first mortal to address it is signing and sealing his own death warrant.' But it was no spirit.

'Our fathers chained in prisons dark, were still in heart and conscience free!' exclaimed Lanty Gorman, and there was no mistaking the voice.

'That you Lanty?' hollered Jimmie Cox, the most daring of our band.

'Who the hell else would it be!' came the reply. 'Get me out of here as quick as you can. Bad luck to Kate McGarrigle! May she die roarin'! When I get my hands on her I'll tear her asunder.'

We fetched the key from Kate and released the prisoner.

'Thanks be to God and to you men!' he blurted out. 'When I thought of bein' locked up there all night, and droves of sufferin' souls comin' and goin', sure I was nearly driven clane out of my mind. Then I thought of screamin', but that would be unseemly in the chapel. So I started to sing the hymn or strive to sing it at any rate. Still I suppose one can't be too sore on Kate. Maybe she was scared to venture up the gallery on the night that was in it and all.'

2

The Trip We Took Over the Mountain

'There's good moonlight in it now, Paddy. Isn't it time we took that trip over the mountain?' John Lawn asked me on our way home from mass one misty Sunday in November.

'Alright. We'll head away the first night there's a nip of frost in the air and no mist swirling up out of the bogholes. We don't want to be wandering round Moor's hill like Johnnie Hump the night the "wee folk" took him.'

'Damn it, you're right, and there's a stray on that mountain too. Didn't William McGuare and Duck Harte go a *shaughran* on it one night when they were comin' back from chasin' after women away around Paddy Arrigle's in Coughlin's town, and never quit till they landed at Tit McGee's of the Finn Hills. Sure the cocks were crowin' and it was clear daylight in the mornin' before either man made it home and hit the scratcher. But I'll make damned sure we won't land at Tit's. I'll bring the compass with me. Man, she's great value to have with you on a strange mountain, or if you were cuttin' scollops on a dark evenin' away in through Mortimer's plantin' or the point of Rossagoale. Sarah brought me the instrument the last time she was home from England. Indeed, there's no house should be without one of them. With a lady like that in your pocket, it would be a long-headed Loughreyman would lead you astray on mountain or in valley.'

We settled for Tuesday night if the fog kept off and after tea-time slipped away in the gathering dusk and were a good mile up Moore's Road before Neil Lawn, wee Jimmie or Cox twigged we had left. There was little fear we'd be followed or that they'd get any bulletin on our movements for some time to come.

Neil would check the cart-house and note that the clarendo bag was missing, but that would only suggest John was away to court in Tonnaghgorm or maybe Tullychurry where high barbed-wire fences had to be negotiated with consequent risks to a man's marriage prospects. Hence, the bag was taken along to cushion the top strand of wire. But John's clarendo bag was an all-purpose one. In it he would carry home the big turkey cock the blond teacher bought for him near Ardara and had transported to Tubber in a turf lorry. It was a fine bird by all accounts and came off a good walk. He was sure to be as fat as a fool come turkey-market time, and John could be lucky enough to lift the couple of pounds profit on him. You had to have the fire full of irons those times before Clement Attlee nationalised the birds of the air and the lilies of the field.

The bird in the hand was a fine thing right enough, but just now John had laid his bird-lime to capture the bird in the bush. Fine well he knew that all the lusty mountain men were clean out of their minds about the big blonde from down the county, and few of them denied that they were under her spell. She was friendly and civil with all of them and never refused to dance with the most splay-footed, but they were thwarted by her aura of superiority when closer contact was sought. The frustration was driving them mad.

John was convinced he had what it took to woo this winsome Marilyn Monroe. He was a little longer in the tooth than the men of the heather and had knocked around a great deal more. Women liked their men to display a degree of maturity and to evince certain debonair qualities when in pursuit of their quarries. John was confident he could rout most rivals in the field, but he still fretted and worried that in the sphere of education he was not her equal.

'It's a devil to be always on guard and watchin' your words', he once confided in me. 'Do you think if I "inged" my endin's more, would it just about tip the scales?'

'No, John', I told him with genuine sincerity. 'If you try that the "ins" will come through like stirabout floating in sweet milk, and you'll make a poultice out of it altogether. Just be yourself and you won't go far wrong.'

Poor John! He never learned that Grainne enjoyed a healthy bear's-hug tackle as well as any other normal girl and that she was fluent in the lip language that does not require words. He was quite excited that he'd be slapping her hand when dealing out for the turkey cock. 'They say feathers are lucky', he declared as we broke our discourse, going in on the edge of McGlinchey's street.

John was heading for Yankee Walshe's of the crossroads to meet the maid, buy the turkey cock and collect the tobacco brought from Ballyshannon by Yankee Walshe for Tom Kelly, the big Lawns and Pat Meehan. These were all neighbours of ours who didn't ride bicycles, seldom went to 'town' (a nickname for Ballyshannon) and did not want to pay the tax imposed on tobacco by a Labour government in Britain.

I was going to *céilí* in McGlinchey's and to listen to the uncrowned queen of the mountain, Una Walshe, who was now on her eighty-fifth year to God. She could weave from the folk memory and the idiom of the people the richest stories to be heard outside the glowing heartland of the Gaeltacht. She had more songs than you could shake a stick at and had no qualms about singing them. When Una held court, time's writ ceased to run.

Una lived with her nephew John McGlinchey, his two sons Peter and John and his daughter Roseanne in a thatched house on a green hillock named Tullagheineaghan, under the shoulder of Breezy Mountain. The McGlincheys were well-read, intelligent folk who could trace the genealogy of every family in the parish and far beyond back for five generations.

The men were still in the byre when we arrived. They had finished milking and were throwing hay to the beasts. John emerged from the byre with two frothy pails of milk. Peter followed after with a puchill full. That would be the foremilk kept for the cat, I knew; foremilk was never given to or drunken by any discerning person. Wasn't the foremilk of a cow or the strippings of a teapot the greatest insult you could offer anyone!

The cat didn't mind. She lurked on the Hugh Martin side of the *seal foscaidh* and waited for the foremilk to be poured into a deep cavity between the flags beyond the door step. Light from the wall lamp fell out them over the half-door, and then Una was unhasping it and advancing to greet me. Hugging and kissing followed and then, '*Céad fáilte romhat, minic nach dtig!*' she greeted me, using the second line of the famous Gaelic salutation.

'*Go raibh máith agat a Úna, a tháisce, acht cad mar gheall ar Sheán s'againne?*' I asked her.

'*Ach, tá seisean ceart go leor. Minic a thig atá ann.*' And then she lapsed into the slave's patter.

'They tell me, John, the Yankee's dog, and indeed every dog in Cashelyard, has quit barking at you!'

'Damn it, Una,' he parried, 'there's nothing unknownst to you. Sure a rooster can't trail his wing at all, but you have every detail down to the colour of the tail feathers. It's a holy sight, surely.'

'She must have great lines of communication altogether', I butted in to relieve the pressure on John.

'If Hitler would have had anything near as good, he'd never have lost the war', John rallied. 'Where do you agents come from at all?'

'O'Connell did better with a knot of straw', she declared. 'Didn't he mobilise the men of Ireland in seven hours once with it!'

'With a knot of straw?' John was puzzled and it showed in his furrowed brow.

'What else?' she reassured him. 'He began in Athlone at sunrise, and before tea-time every able-bodied man in the kingdom had got his summons. The message fanned out from the centre, and within seven hours every man from Mizen Head to Malin and from Howth Head to Black Sod was mobilised.'

'And what happened then?' John asked, his curiosity aroused.

'No orders came to march, and so the great hosting never took place.'

'Ah, the ol' bugger! He wouldn't stand up to the English when the chips were down! I wonder was there any truth in the crack that he invented a machine to beget children by steam?'

'I hope you'll not be depending on a steam engine when you and the school-teacher throw your old duds together.'

But John waited for no more. He was off through the gap at the gable-end of the house that led to the near-cut across the fields to Yankee Walshe's, and you couldn't catch a rabbit on its own pad.

'Come on away in', Una invited me. John and the milk pails followed after us.

'Here, Roseanne. Take this milk away and strain it. I must clean myself up.' There was an iron pot hooked to a cleek that hung from the crane crook. It was boiling and every time the lid was lifted the kitchen filled with an aroma that made your teeth water. There were at least two or three cock chickens cooking there. Potatoes were cooking in another pot that seemed as large as the great Famine pot they had on display for many years on the holy island of Lough Derg. When the potatoes were ready Peter teamed them into a large sally-rod basket supported by a bucket that stood in the middle of the floor. Steam enveloped the kitchen and swirled out over the half-door. The water the potatoes had been boiled in was used for washing the feet of revellers who had a big night's dancing before them, but the McGlincheys would not be going dancing this night and had a guest to entertain.

As Roseanne busied herself with the preparation of the evening meal, Una took her cue from the steaming potatoes.

'The time of the run-away matches,' she began, 'the young girl always ran out in the smoke of the teamed spuds. Romeo would be waiting near the byre door and they'd escape to a relative's house and send word back that they had run away. All repaired to the relative's house, and there was singing and dancing until clear daylight next morning with lashings and leavings to eat and drink. This did away with the haggling and horse-trading that went on when matches were made and the groom looked for a dowry. Cupid should have a wee say in such matters. It takes him to put the head-sheaf on a marriage. Indeed, mine wasn't a made match, but still I didn't come to Mick Kerrigan empty handed.'

Una had been married to a man by the name of Kerrigan, long since dead. They had had no children.

'The teaming of the spuds and the run-away romance always puts me in mind of the old song, *The Trip We Took Over the Mountain*. How's this it goes? Oh, aye!' She threw back her head, shut her eyes and began:

THE TRIP WE TOOK OVER THE MOUNTAIN
One night as the moon luminated the sky
I first took a notion I'd marry
I put on my hat and away I did hie
You would think that I was in a hurry.
When I came to that spot where I often had been
My heart gave a jump when my charmer I seen
I lifted the latch and I bade her good e'en
'Will you trip with me over the mountain?'

'What humour is this you've got into your head?
Still I'm glad for a while to be near you
It's twelve of the clock and they're all gone to bed
Speak low or my mother will hear you.'
'I've spoken my mind and I never will rue
I've courted a year and I think that will do
But if you refuse me, sweet maiden adieu
And I go back alone o'er the mountain.'

She looked at me long, and then heaved a deep sigh
She trembled, a little unsteady

Then rubbed out the tear she was going to cry
'In God's name, my darling, get ready!'
'Just wait for a minute till I get my shoes.'
My heart gave a lep when I heard the glad news
She lifted the latch saying, 'I hope you'll excuse
My simplicity over the mountain.'

At that time the moon was gone down in the west
And the morning star brightly was shining
We both made the journey with greatest of haste
And got wed at the alter of Hymen.
In peace and contentment we spent the long day
The anger of parents it soon wore away
And often we chat when there's little to say
Of the trip we took over the mountain.

When the meal was over we settled down to a heavy seam
of singing and story-telling.
'Have you ever heard a story, Paddy, that came from
Brockagh side, or maybe round the Croaghs country, about
a spinning hag? I heard the ol' sockman from Carrick at it
long years ago. He used to come round here selling socks
and gloves and woolies of that kind. He always stopped
here when he came south of Barnesmore or east of Laghey.
'Course he told it in Irish. His English wasn't the best.'
'Sean Ban Mac Meniman mentions a spinner in one of his
books. He called her Cailleach na h-Olna, I think.'
'That's the one, I'm sure. She came back one All Souls'
Night to finish some spinning she promised to do before
death took her. Now I have a song here about a hag who
used to spin, but if the song is telling the truth, she could
have been a witch as well. Here it is. It's in the slave's patter,
as you say:

THE HAG'S RANT
When we thought we'd get sowans for supper
We struck up a lilt of a song

The old hag she croaks up in the corner
'It's time that the tollies were on
Oh, the tollies, the tollies
Oh, the tollies', said she.
'Let them be wee ones or big ones
A wee drop of porridge for me.'

The spuds, they were teamed on the basket
We all gathered round for a feed
The old crone kept spinning and grinning
She didn't pay very much heed.
I looked to the crock where the cream was
Old Susie, she chuckled with glee
'They tell me that hunger's good kitchen
So eat them up dry, boys', said she.

I've heard of old hags milking tethers
And a *cailleach* they found in the churn
But that old crone hunched up in the corner
Some day at a witch stake will burn.
The *bean an tí* is dropping her stitches
Old Susie is nodding her head
And Lanty's unlacing his britches
It's time dacent folk were in bed.

Right fol did dee ol did ee aarl
Right fol did dee ol did a dee
Right fol did ee ol did ee aarl
If only old Ireland was free!

'Do you still spin, Una?' I asked her.
'Well, I don't now, Paddy. Not a bit good telling lies about
it, but the sight's not as good as it used to be. And then there's
no one can card wool for me and it's hell to control the cards
when the rheumity pains tie knots on your knuckles. Do you
mind the fortnight you were here when you were still in the
short trousers? I used to have you carding then. And a right
hand you were at it, too. You were taking down stories and

songs from me all day and then at night I was teaching you
to card.'

'I suppose there's none of the hand-loom weavers left
round these parts now, Una?'

'I'm afraid not. There's weavers away down round Ardara
and Kilcar, but even there I doubt if you'd get one of them
who could weave the makings of a shirt out of lint. Oh, the
Lagan men did well out of the lint during the war. There
were water-driven scutch-mills in plenty. One on every burn,
nearly; but the tow was being bought up for the war effort,
across in England. Things are not so rosy since Hitler threw
in the towel. Still, we're not so bad. We have our own heather
besoms, the wild bees and the odd moorcock to cackle in its
sleep when night settles in round the mountain streams. Did
you ever hear a song, Paddy, they called *Bonnie Lass Among the
Heather*?'

'Damn it, I don't think so. That's one I haven't got. Can
you sing it?'

BONNIE LASS AMONG THE HEATHER
Oh! as I roved out one morn, sure 'tis well I do
    remember
I was heading for a fair in the ripe month of September
I met a damsel gay, and we tripped along together
And she stole my heart away, bonnie lass among the
    heather, Oh!

I said, 'My heart's delight, have you come to drive me
    crazy
Since your vision crossed my sight, sure my mind is
    most unaisy
I will buy your year-old yoes and the ram you've on the
    tether
If you'll come and live with me, and forget the blooming
    heather, Oh!

'On by lush land cattle browse around manor and
    Drumoghill

And you're hunched up in the knowes where old men
  on crutches haughle
Down below, wild youth abound and they strive and
  throng together
And there's rakes of level ground, if you leave the
  blooming heather, Oh!'

'Kind sir,' the maid replied, 'you can keep your land
  and money
For your wealth's no match for pride and the wild bees
  love their honey
I'm as happy as can be with my father and my mother
And it would take a canny blade for to win me from the
  heather, Oh!'

When Una tired and the lulls between songs and stories
lengthened, the slow, measured ticking of the wag-o'-the-
wall marked the return to the fray of old Father Time.

Then the hoary old timepiece gave a rusty wheeze and
struck the midnight hour. The man of the house reached
for his beads that hung on the brace and began the rosary.
We joined him. I was relieved when he opted for the 'Hail
Holy Queen' and the 'Litany of Loreto' after only five decades, but when he launched into the trimmings the net
was cast far and wide. He prayed for Christians, pagans
and Jews, heathens, Hindus and Mahommedans, the people of Ireland, our dead, our exiles and our government.
Fianna Fail ruled the roost then. Lastly, he appealed to
the high courts of heaven that we be given a favourable
judgement.

I thanked the Lord I was wearing heavy winter trousers,
for a lengthy spell kneeling on a flagged kitchen floor is a
milder method of knee-capping. Why not coin a word and
call it 'flagation'? Una and John senior bade us goodnight
and went to bed. The young ones sat on and cracked away
about old times.

'Will you be having a card play this winter?' I inquired.

'No,' John replied, 'it's too much of a hassle. Setting up three tables in the kitchen here and one in the room is a lot of bother. Then there's the feeding of sixty or seventy players, maybe four times. Add to that the loss of a night's sleep and it's damned near as bad as a wake! And of course there's women in this house say a pack of cards is the devil's prayer book.'

'Arah, quit me now! Do you mean to tell me, Roseanne, you heed old pishrogues like that?' I admonished the lady in question.

'It's hard to say, Paddy. If cards are played properly and honestly I suppose there's not a gra'deal of harm in them. But I firmly believe that the minute the "good boys" start cheating, the ol' boy puts the big, cloven *spag* across the threshold.'

'It's a sin the card-playing has gone out of favour', I said. 'Many's the good night's gambling we had in the thirties. I mind my father and Big Hughie McGuaran taking me to a twenty-five drive in Bannagh Hall that Father O'Flannigan, the parish priest, was running. We cycled up and it was a fierce, wet night. Damn, the bit word was about the devil prowling around either. Some man did put a pack of parish cards in his pocket and Father Flannigan nearly raised the rigging of the hall, roaring on us to examine our conscience. He never got his pack of cards and still no devil appeared. Wouldn't you think stealing was a worse crime than cheating!'

'We saw some good nights here at card-plays. Sure you were at one yourself. Your father and Jimmie Cox were with you', Peter McGlinchey joined in the discussion.

'I mind it well', I said. Hugh Cavanagh from Cashelyard was here and he never quit about going off to Spain to fight for Christ. It be to be during the Spanish Civil War.'

'He only wanted to hear himself speaking. Sure the Cavanaghs were all staunch Fianna Failers', John interjected.

'Old Tommie Tow Whiskers was here too and Big Jim Walshe from the Lough', I probed.

'Aye, and Mickie McCafferty from the Derries.'

'Was he the old fellow who was always gerning and chandering about the stranger not getting fair do?' I asked.

'The very bucko. He was the scourge of every twenty-five drive from Creevy to Biddy's O' Barnes and every gambling match from Frosses to Finnmore. He'd eat you alive without salt if you were his partner and lost a trick', John declared.

'Where is he now?' I asked innocently.

'I'm afraid I wouldn't know. Gone where the good gamblers go, I suppose. And these women say that cards or card-playing is not allowed in heaven. Poor Mickie would be hard put if they wouldn't let him deal a hand', John concluded.

John Lawn lifted the latch and walked in, heavily laden with the spoils of war. He bore on his back in the fabled clarendo bag a giant turkey cock, in his pocket countless half-quarters of Warhorse tobacco for his neighbours in Scardan and Garvery, and in his heart the goodwill, if not the love, of the blond bombshell from Ardara.

The moon still shone brightly so we retraced our steps over the mountain to the valleys and drumlins of Mulleek.

3

Hiúdaí Pháidí Hiúdaí

The nights lengthened. The cold intensified and itchy feet tormented me again. A niggling restlessness gnawed at my vitals. I must be off, over the hills and far away.

I would go to the Eastern World and breathe the fragrance of Arabian gales, do great deeds of valour and maybe rescue the odd damsel in distress. Don Quixote was too long dead. It was high time another knight set out to make a fool of himself that live men might laugh again. The dead could bury the dead, as Christ said once.

Men needed to laugh great bellows of ribald, Rabelaisian laughter to dispel the gloomy fear and foreboding of postwar pessimism.

And I'd be following in the footsteps of heroes immortalised in the sagas of the past. Admittedly, most of them were giants; but then Cuchuliann was a small man and Napoleon was not exactly a six-footer.

True, I had no *gae bolga* to disembowel my enemies and no means of recruiting three hundred thousand men to head off on a skiing expedition over the frozen alps. I dreaded ice. It was the stumbling block of most Ulstermen. We could not escape the shadow cast by the Titanic. Avalanches were wild handlings altogether.

So I settled for Dublin and a stint at the university in the hope that I could earn a crust more by the furrow of my brow than by the sweat of it. Padraig O'Connaire had once warned us to keep clear of work. It was the curse of God, he maintained, and hence to be shunned at all cost.

I managed somehow to combine studies at Earlsfort Terrace with those of Francha House, Crumlin Road, where Maeve

Ní Dhúgáin and Hiúdaí Pháidí Hiúdaí O'Duibheannaigh
handed us the key to our Gaelic heritage. This little island
owes them a great debt that can never be repaid.

Hiúdaí had a priceless store of songs in Irish. One of the
finest was *'Geaftaí Bhaile Atha Buí'*, or in the slave's patter,
The Gates of Ballaghbuoy. I give it here:

GEAFTAÍ BHAILE ATHA BUÍ

*Ag geaftaí Bhaile Atha Buí, a rinne mise an gníomh a bhí
    amaideach baoth-déanta*

*Ealú le mnaoi seal tamaill ins an oíche ar neamnchead a rabh
    faoi na spéarthai*

*Bhí mé lag gan brí, gan misneach in mo chroí is í agam ar
    mín-shléibhe;*

*Bhí an codladh a mo chloíd agus b'éigin damhsa luí agus
    d'imigh sí ina fíorhaighdean.*

*'Gabhail a luí don ghrian faoin am seo aréir nach agamsa bhí
    an scéal buartha*

*Ba é a shamhailt damhsa an té a shínfí ins an chré O is a
    Mhuire nach mé an trua*

*Is é 'déarfadh mo chairde, an méid a bhí i láthair: 'Altaigh leas
    na mná, a bhuachaill.'*

*Is an meid a ngoilfadh orthu mo chas, goilfeadh siad a sá fá mo
    chroí a bheith mo lár ina ghual dubh.*

*Dá mbeinnse thall sa Spainn i mo luí ar leaba an bháis agus
    cluinimse do dháil in Éirinn*

*Go n-éireoinn chomh samh leis an bhradán ar an tsnámh
    induibheagán i lár na h-Eirne*

*Focal ar bith mná ní chreidfidh mé go brath Mura bhfaighidh
    mise scriofá i mBéarla é*

*Gur chaith mé naoi lá ag cleasaiocht leis an bhás ag dúil go
    bhfaighinn spás ar éigin.*

*Is agamsa atá an mháistreas is measa i gcríocha Fail cé gur
    soineanta clár a h-éadáin*

Chuirfeadh sí mo chás ibhfad agus i ngearr agus b'fhurasta ar

chas a réiteach
An madadh rua bheith sách, an chaora dhubh ar fáil is ní
   chluinfi mé go brath ag éileamh
Agus m'fhocal duit a Sheáin, go bhfuil ealaíon ins na mna agus
   codail fein go samh ina n-eamais.

THE GATES OF BALLAGHBUOY

At the gates of Ballaghbuoy, like Paris back in Troy
I did perpetrate a deed of dark unreason
I led a lass astray; on the mountains with her lay
Without leave or licence, surely 'twas a treason.
Then lacked the thrust and power to storm that maiden's
   bower
My vapid wooing won but hate and scorning
Till overcome with sleep, I sank in slumber deep
And she left me, still a virgin in the morning.

As the sun sank big and bright, about this time last
   night
'Twas I who looked a sight of woe and sorrow
Like a corpse that courts decay when stretched out in
   the clay
Oh! Mary, bring me comfort on tomorrow.
The friends I meet by day confuse me when they say
'Bless womenfolk, and never blight or hinder.'
But it grieves their hearts full sore to see me at death's
   door
And the heart that blazed with love a burned out cinder.

Were I beyond in Spain, on deathbead stretched in pain
And were told your bed with me you'd soon be sharin'
I'd rise with redder blood than the salmon in the flood
As it leaps up Asseroe back on the Erne.
Word of womenbreed I won't hearken to or heed
Till it's printed in the tongue of the invader
For nine nights I diced with death, and gasped and
   strove for breath
And at length won back the ground to rout the raider.

And now for life I'm cursed with the woman who is
   the worst
In the four shores of the land, though she looks civil
Our tangled wool I fear, she's carding far and near
But at snarling up fine thread she's the divil.
The fat and well-fed fox, the ram among the rocks
You seldom hear the likes of them complaining
So, dear John, take my advice, with woman do not
   splice
Sleep sound in peace, a single man remaining.

Hiúdaí taught me many other fine Gaelic songs, but the
one that haunted me for many moons, because of its heart-
break and unutterable loneliness was *Tá Mé 'Mo Shuí*. Brian
O'Rourke, the Galway scholar, claims that it is a Mayo song
because of its reference to *Béal An Átha*. One should not
be too dogmatic about the mention of place names when
determining a song's origin. There are a goodly number of
places known as *Béal An Átha* throughout Ireland. In fact,
there is one near Gortahork, County Donegal, and it is at
the mouth of the River Atha! Indeed, both Hiúdaí Pháidí
Hiúdaí and old Master Gillespie, who knew the *seanchas* of
the Clochaneely parish off by heart, always maintained that
this song originated in Gortahork. Even today the locals will
point to the spot where the banshee and the poet met.

Tá Mé 'Mo Shuí
Tá mé 'mo shuí ó d'éirigh an ghealach aréir
Ag cur tine thios gan sgith, is dá fadú go gear
Tá bunadh a' tí 'na luí agus tá mise liom féin
Tá na coiligh ag glaoch is an tír 'na gcodladh acht mé.

A sheacht n-anam deag do bheal, do mhalaidh 's do ghruaidh
Do shúil ghorm-ghle fa'r threig mé aiteas is suairc
Le cumhaidh 'do dheidh ní léir damh an bealach a shiúl
'S a charaid mo chleibh, tá sléibhte eadar mé agus tú.

Deiridh lucht léinn gur cloite an galar an gradh

Char admuigh mé é go rabh sé i ndeidh mo chroí 'stoigh a
  chradh
Aicid ro-ghear, faraor, nar sheachnuigh mé í
Is go gcuireann sí arraing is céad fríd cheart-lár mo chroí.

Casadh bean-sí damh thíos ag Lios Bhéal an Atha
D'fhiafruigh mé dí an sgaoilfeadh glas ar bith gradh
Is duairt sí 'gcois íseal i mbriathraibh soineannta sáimh
Nuair a théid sé fa'n chroí cha sgaoiltear as é go brath.

I AM AWAKE

I am awake since the moon crossed the mountain last
  night
The fires I've kindled have dwindled to *greeshagh*
  red-bright
The rest of the household's asleep, but I weep on alone
The rooster is crowing, not knowing the cause of my
  moan.

The blessings of God on your brow and the red of your
  mouth
Your eyes blue and bright like the sky kissed by sun in
  the south
For love unrequitted I'm blighted and driven astray
And the mountains now rear up between us to darken
  the way.

The sages maintain that love's pain is a strength-sapping
  plague
I do not deny that it aches like a colic or ague
There was no escape when it struck and I woke with a
  start
And a hundred and one piercing arrows shot straight
  through my heart.

Down Lisballina way I met a banshee with blue eyes
I begged and beseeched her love's leech from my poor
  heart to prize

She spoke soft and low, 'It's a woe that will waste
you away
When it pierces the heart it will smart until crack of
Doomsday.'

The Kerryman scanned the pages of my poems carefully
and gave them back to me. ''Tis good', he said, 'in fact, very
good, but definitely not *Bell* material. Send them to Father
Senan. He'll probably use them in the *Capuchin Annual*.'

Then I began talking. Old Paddy Rooney, *Bell* office manager, had just introduced us. He excused himself and made a
speedy exit. We faced each other on the steep office steps.

'So you're Séamus de Faoite? I recognised you from that
photograph in the *Capuchin Annual* away back in 1943. That
was a smashing story. 'Spring Thrush', or something, you called
it? In fact it was the only available reading on my first hour
in King's College, Belfast. The attendant had been very con-
siderate. He could have given me last week's *Belfast Telegraph*,
he said, but I being a Taig and all might not like its tone.

'Then, when I went to take the air, another student who
evinced kleptomaniac proclivities swiped the *Annual*. The
confounded creature couldn't even read! When I reported
the matter to the authorities, the poor fellow got three days
bread and water in the "flowery dell."'

Maybe I had been overbearing. In hindsight, I surely was
indiscreet. Then I went on and attempted to set him afire with
the burning zeal to Gaelicise Ireland that consumed my soul
at that time. 'We'd have to restore a high king on Tara and
four other provincial kings. There would be one at Cashel
in Munster, one at Allen in Leinster, where Fionn MacCool
once ruled the roost. Connaught would have its king, too,
at Cruachan in Rosscommon, and of course the Ulster king
would reign from Aileach!'

The man from the Reeks stared at me steadily but said not
a word. This did not worry me unduly. No Munsterman took
a native of Ulster for granted since Cuchuliann tricked Cu Ree

Ard Mac Daire An Oir into the streamlet to be drowned in a torrent of sour milk. No sir, Kerrygold butter was game ball at all times, but beware of the Munster buttermilk!

I had gone to the *Bell* office in the first instance to find out what befell my book-token prize of one guinea that I had won in the literary competition organised by a columnist known as the Bellman. Competitors were asked to name the twenty best novels in the English language. My list had lifted the award, but no book-token ever reached me. Paddy Rooney assured me it had been mailed out to my address, but the postal services were so poor in both ends of our island that perhaps it had been mislaid or even lost. However, since it had not got my length he would have another sent. His memory was bad. I have not yet received my book-token.

But he did give me a most useful little textbook on public health and sanitary law that was very handy indeed when I was studying for my diploma in public health.

As we descended the office steps we came face to face with the associate editor of the *Bell*, as Seamus was then. Peadar O'Donnell was editor and owner also, I believe. O'Faolan and O'Connor had gone off to write masterpieces.

So began a friendship that lasted until Seamus was laid in the clay of a graveyard on the outskirts of Dublin City where the larks he loved so well still soar and sing.

Next day was Saturday. Lectures were over early. I went into town to get some books and was standing in a queue in Duleer Street waiting for a 50A bus when Seamus joined me. It was then we discovered that we were living on the same road. We sat together in the bus and he told me excitedly of a short story he had begun writing that very morning. 'New World's Eve' it was to be called. It was a beautiful piece of writing, almost poetry in fact, in which it was proclaimed that 'the blare of brass was the blare of glory'.

For both of us it could be said we were standing on the doorstep of the New World. I don't think either of us ever crossed the threshold. We were fiercely loyal to the old stock and had only contempt for the Micky Mouse men who ran around waving flags and shouting meaningless words, mostly in the slave's patter. They strove and heaved and grunted but failed to raise the stone. Sooner than break our girths in helping them we chose to reign our steeds round and return to the hidden Ireland. If ever the little fellows discovered it, they would die of intellectual indigestion.

Seamus was a loyal friend. He tempered my extreme views and pared away my prejudices. No man knew better that too long a sacrifice can make a stone of the heart, and so he strove tirelessly to inch away the steel in mine and to get blood flowing again in the arteries. I became almost as enthusiastic about his short stories as he was himself and can claim to have been at the conception, if not the birth, of the best of them.

There was 'Kate's Grandchild', 'Pictures in a Pawnshop', 'The Day Mary Clare Met the Bishop', 'The Old Stock', 'The American Apples', 'Law Abiding', 'Moon Road Home', 'The Boot', 'The King is Dead', 'Dry Train', 'The Nun', and 'The More We are Together'. He wrote one splendid play, *The Night of the Moon*. In fact, it was entrusted to me by his wife, Eileen, after his death. Perhaps the Druid Theatre has the flair and poetic vision to produce it. I doubt if any other theatre in this island would have the ability to give it the treatment it deserves.

The *Bell* folded up in May. I had obtained my diploma and was hanging around Dublin in the hope that I'd get some holiday relief work. There was none forthcoming. Seamus was for a short period of time out of work. Finally, he joined the staff of the *Irish Independent*. During our period of enforced idleness we went for long walks out by the green hills and on to Tallaght. It's all built up now.

We carried two walking-sticks and these seemed to generate a degree of excitement amongst the children playing hop-scotch or swinging on a rope from a lamppost. They followed us for part of the way, their eyes dancing with devilment.

They did not seem eager to make our acquaintance but were keen to get on at least speaking terms with our sticks.

'Hello walking-sticks! Hello walking-sticks!' they chanted

again and again as they tripped and skipped around us. We ignored them and strode out with an air of dignity and gentility that very quickly repelled and overawed them. I often thought it was a sin to kill their fun and frolicking, but then it is dangerous to allow baiting of any kind to develop.

Dogs also took a dislike to our walking-sticks and were wont to bark loud and long at our approach, but none of them attempted to savage us. Perhaps they were too well bred or too well trained to go so far.

It was during those long walks that our literary masterpieces were planned and plotted. Seamus fulfilled that early promise but I can only say I am still trying. I left Dublin for the wide, open country in July, but was called back to work there in November.

The old friendship was renewed and on the Whitsuntide weekend of the following summer we headed out on an excursion to Killarney, de Faoite's own town. His parents were still alive, old stock to the marrow. I doubt if ever I met a couple so near to the threshold of heaven. I was shown the tree whereon grew 'The American Apples', the lane where the old woman in 'Kate's Grandchild' lived, and the cathedral spire as high as gull flight and the rhododendrons immortalised in 'Mansion Purples'. It was like a journey to the land of heart's desire.

On the way down, an itinerant minstrel boarded the train at Rathmore. He played on a tin whistle or, to be more correct, played with it. To say he was bad would be an understatement. He was the worst tin whistler I ever heard and that includes Tom Farrell at a Saint Patrick's Day fair in Belleek and wee Willie Doherty trying to play three whistles at the one time in a Derry pantomime. There was an English tourist on the train. It was his first visit to Ireland. He got all worked up. 'Blimey! a Kerry piper, a Kerry piper!' squeaked the innocent abroad who evidently had a record of John McCormick singing *The Days of the Kerry Dances*, or who was maybe an avid reader of *Punch* and came to the kingdom to hunt for leprechauns and banshees.

Seamus was driven to patriotic wrath. He rose to his feet and denounced the imposter.

'That's no Kerry piper', he told all and sundry. 'He's a Cork City beggar legalising his vagrant ways by tuttling on a tin whistle.' The wretch had just limped his way through *Buttons and Bows* and was striving to go *South of the Border, Down Mexico Way*. None of these tunes would be included in the repertoire of a Kerry piper.

'Shall we make a whip of cords, Seamus?' I ribbed him.

'Tis alright, Paddy,' he assured me, 'but I detest deception of any kind, even if 'tis an Englishman is being deceived.'

Seamus was a master of the art and craft of the short story, surely the most gifted we'd had since O'Connor and O'Faolain. Strange that only one volume of his short stories has been published. I refer of course to *The More We are Together*, published posthumously.

Surely it is time that those of us who knew him well got together and insisted that the short stories not listed in that book be given to the Irish people in book form.

4

In Kerry Long Ago

In 1950 I set sail for Kerry to take up my first permanent post as public health officer. I was in good company down there. Paddy McAndrew from Mayo, surely one of nature's greatest gentlemen, ruled in Tralee's urban area with undisputed sway. Next to the breathtaking beauty of the Reeks, he loved nothing better than traditional songs and music. Paddy Burke of Milltown, one of the finest full forwards ever graced the green and gold, and that includes Bomber Liston, worked south Kerry and north Kerry, and the Dingle Peninsula was assigned to me.

In those distant days we were not overworked. Aodh de Blacam, operating as director of publicity in Doctor Noel Browne's dynamic department of health, decided that the humble little house fly, otherwise known as *musco domestica*, was the principal carrier of infectious diseases in our island.

War on the house fly was declared. DDT, both in liquid and powder form, wreaked havoc amongst the insects and their breeding grounds. However, to get home to the adult population the menace of dunghills, middens, dumps and any or all accumulations of dirt and filth and their attendant fly infestation, it was necessary to recruit the school children as shock troops.

With this end in view, colourful booklets were printed by de Blacam's section of the department and sent down to the health sections of county councils for distribution amongst school pupils and students. It was amazing the impact this campaign made even on sophisticated folk like the Kerry people. My brief was to go along to the schools and lecture or chat to the pupils about the mighty atom monsters known as house flies, and I must say I enjoyed every minute of it.

Don't blame me when you hear that those lively little pep talks generally ended in singing and story-telling recitals. Bryan McMahon, novelist, playwright, balladeer, short-story writer and school master par excellence, was in reality the culprit. He spread the news around that the inspector was a smashing singer of the ballad and the traditional song and had great time for the ancient pieties. Maybe there was no evidence of the red carpet, but I can assure you the welcome I got was a royal one indeed.

The pattern of events was as follows. I gave a short, incisive talk on the menace of the house fly. This was succeeded by a question time relating to the habits, haunts and breeding grounds of these detestable insects.

'Where do you find house flies?'

'On the winda', sir.'

'On the dunghill, sir', a more daring boy would shout.

'In the tilet, sir', another sang out.

The 'tilet' to them was the latrine or pail closet that was the only sanitary convenience in rural schools until Neil Blaney became minister for local government and piped water supplies and sewerage facilities were made available even in the wildest and remotest glens and valleys of the twenty-six counties. When the distribution of the coloured booklets depicting the evil house fly fizzing off on a raid, with a tank of deadly poison on his back, had been completed and the pupils were abuzz with excitement and a burning zeal to demolish dungheaps, middens and other accumulation or deposits of dirt, it was time for the singing teacher to put the school choir, or just maybe the best singing class, through its paces. Then my cow was in the pound.

They hollered for *The Valley of Knockanure, Roddy McCurley* and *The Mountains of Pomeroy* and would settle for nothing less than *Moorlough Mary* or *Lough Erne Shore*. These were genuine, bardic sessions and introduced a colourful subject into the rather dull school curriculum. Bryan McMahon was well ahead of his time in the field of education.

Many and varied were the pastimes available to the man of leisure abroad in Kerry in that golden age. There was good trout fishing, blood-tingling Gaelic football games, the swapping of songs and stories with Bryan McMahon and Eamonn Kelly, and the time-honoured task of rescuing fair damsels in distress. It goes without saying that this hobby was the most enjoyable of them all. In the kingdom of Kerry, you see, all the young maidens are princesses. There was Tilly from Brandon, whose dark tresses cascaded like the velvet dusk of a June night over the white marble of her shoulders. There was the sloe-eyed, mantillaed Mary from Caherciveen, whose ordinary speech was like a well-sung love lyric. There was the little girl on the way from Listowel to Glountane, whose granny warned her to beware of the strange Northerner. 'He could be a communist!' she counselled her. It was the only time I was taken for a Russian.

On most Saturday evenings Paddy McAndrew went over to Milltown to *céilí* with old John Burke or to have his car serviced with Paddy Slattery, the garage man. Paddy could tune an engine so fine that you'd scarcely hear her purr.

I recall with deep affection a Saturday night spent in that mid-Kerry village in heroic company. The super from Tralee and the local Garda sergeant had been drinking all day. The latter had been an old IRA man in his day. We joined them, and a singing session was soon underway. *Tipperary So Far Away*; *The Foggy Dew* . . . 'Twas England bade the wild geese go that small nations might be free'; *The Tri-Coloured Ribbon*; *Kelly, the Boy from Killane* . . . 'And the banshee cried where our heroes died in the valley of Knockanure.' If I sang it once I must have sung it seven times that memorable night. If Bryan McMahon had never written another line, he would be remembered forever wherever green is worn.

No other ballad inspired by the war for independence evokes the pain and poignance, the pride and *mórtas cine* of a people rising from the dead to shake off the chains of bondage:

THE VALLEY OF KNOCKANURE

You may sing and speak of Easter week and the heroes
    of ninety-eight
Of the fearless men who roamed the glen for victory or
    defeat
There were those who died on the green hillside, they were
    outlawed on the moor
Not a word was said of the gallant dead in the valley of
    Knockanure.

There was Dalton, Walshe and Lyons, boys, they were
    young and in their pride
In every house, in every crowd, they were always side
    by side
The republic bold they did uphold, though outlawed on
    the moor
And side by side they fought and died in the valley of
    Knockanure.

It was on an autumn evening these three young men lay
    down
To wait upon a brief dispatch to come from Tralee town
It wasn't long till Lyons came on saying, 'Time isn't mine
    nor your'
But alas! 'twas late and they met their fate in the valley
    of Knockanure.

Upon a neighbouring hillside we listened in calm dismay
In every house for miles around a maiden knelt to pray
They're closing in around them now, with rifle fire so
    sure
And Dalton's dead and Walshe is down in the valley of
    Knockanure.

For they brought them hence beyond a fence wherein
     the furze did bloom
Like brothers so they faced the foe to meet their vengeful
     doom
When Dinny spoke his voice it broke with a passion
     proud and pure
'For our land we die as we face the sky in the valley of
     Knockanure.'

There they lay on the damp, cold clay, martyred for
     Ireland's cause
Where the cowardly clan of the Black and Tans has
     shown them England's laws
No more they'll feel the soft breeze steal o'er uplands
     fresh and pure
For the wild geese fly where the heroes lie in the valley
     of Knockanure.

As the evening sun was sinking beyond the Feale and Lee
The pale moon was rising 'way out beyond Tralee
The glistening stars shone bright afar and gleamed over
     Cullen's moor
And the banshee cried where our heroes died in the
     valley of Knockanure.

I met with Dalton's mother, and these words to me
     did say
'May the Lord have mercy on my son, who fell in the
     fight today
Could I but kiss his cold, cold lips my aching heart
     'twould cure
And I'd gladly lay him down to rest in the valley of
     Knockanure.'

Rat! tat! tat! tat! rang the loud knocking on the pub door.
'The Bunann Buis, the bloody Bunann Buis!' roared the
sergeant. 'Out! Out! Every man jack of oo!'
     The Bunann Buis were two leggy young fellows originally

from some boggy swamp in the Midlands. Their long, thin trams and the suggestion of a forward lean gave them the look of wading birds. Both of them had red hair and vile tempers. They were consumed with a desire to make Ireland sober and sported two big pioneer pins like the shield of Connor MacNessa. They would have booked the super as quickly as any other sinner found on the licenced premises.

We poured out into the back yard and braved the barbed-wire of the boundary fence between the publican and Paddy Slattery. All of us but one succeeded in crossing the top strand of barbed-wire. The only casualty was the super. His best trousers got snarled up in the barbs, at considerable risk to his marriage prospects for, like myself, he was still footloose and fancy-free. We went to his aid with a step-ladder and I am pleased to relate that he was extricated without the necessity to send for either tailor or surgeon.

We slipped silently into Paddy Flaherty's kitchen. Salmon was plentiful, for the Lammas floods had come early. There were two fine fish boiling in a metal pot on the range and Mrs Flaherty didn't delay long in laddling large portions on to plates for the belated visitors.

The Bunanns were forced to return to the stations with their tails between their legs and we restarted our singing session. Old John Burke was finishing the ballad extolling the architecture of the tomb he had built for himself, where he would lie in state and survey the tinkers passing to the Fair of Puck, when Peter called the rolls and called him home as dawn peeped in through the curtains. We headed back for Ballynullen Terrace, Tralee, well satisfied with the night's crack.

On another Sunday when there were no inter-county football games being played, I joined Paddy McAndrew and his good wife on a visit to the Gap of Dunloe. We called into Kate Kearney's cottage for refreshments before I would mount a white steed and gallop away to *Tír na n-Óg* through the Gap of Dunloe. It was a very small establishment at that time but it had character all of its own. Paddy said they pulled a good pint there too. As he blew away the froth from the rim of the glass and Mrs MacAndrew went off to powder her nose, I stole a glance round the cottage. There were a few English tourists sipping tea morosely at a small table and up front of the bar stood a Yankee officer in full uniform.

He was being entertained by a dapper little man wearing a battered velour hat and carrying a hunting horn in his right hand. There was no doubt whatsoever the little man had completely mesmerised the big GI by his antics.

He was composing doggerel and proclaiming it at the loud of his head as I came within earshot:

The groves of Blarney and sweet Killarney
And my brother Barney all Boston bound
He was losht for ages where wild water rages
But in history's pages he at lasht was found.
In the White House shittin' like a Persian kitten
That had losht its mitten in a bag of male
On a mishty morn, going round the horn, he wash
Shipwrecked badly in a windy gale.

'Could wild Will Shakespeare or the mighty Homer write anything nearly as good as that!'

'Gee, it's fine, really fine! And I must tell you I sure do appreciate good poetry. But sir, can you sing *Danny Boy*?'

'Old Doyle is no shinger', he told the Yank. 'He's a rechiter. Some muttered of McMurragh, who brought the Norman o'er Shome, cursed him with Iscariot, that day in Baltimore with one great howling, growling roar. No more! No more! Arah! I'll drink it. Shure you might as well be drunk ashe the way oo are! Up Kerry! Come on away out to the sunshine and I'll show oo a trick or two.'

We followed him out. In truth it was a beautiful day. You could see clearly into the purple depths of the Gap. 'Attention

pay me, my countrymen and shitizens of the world! I'm goin'
to blow this horn. If you hear it echo once, you'll have great
good luck. If you hear it re-echo you'll have great, great good
luck, but if you hear it re-echo twice or thrice you'll have
great, great, grand good luck.'

He blew his horn loudly. I heard it echo and re-echo at
least seven times away up in the Gap and down in the Black
Valley on the other side and told him so.

'*D'anam chun diabhal*!' he exclaimed. 'You're a favoured son
of Adam. Step forward, good luck grandee.' I obeyed. 'Here's
a sprig of white heather and cross my palm with shilver. A
half-crown will do.'

I reached him the half-crown. 'Good', he commented. 'Now
stoop down and look out through your ashe and you'll shee
the fairies headin' for the Fair of Puck.'

'But the fair's still a fortnight away!' I reminded him.

'That doeshn't matter. The wee folk have nothin' to learn.
They arrive early and shtake their claim to "gentle" campin'
ground before the tinkers gather. No tinker would pitch
camp on "gentle" ground. When he sees the flint heads
scattered around, he wouldn't come next or near the place
in case his animals would get elf-shot. Oh, cute boyos the
shame little folk!'

I stooped down and looked out through my legs but
neither hilt nor hair of the *sluagh shee* was in sight. I
crossed the road and approached an osler who was holding
a seventeen-hands-high steed by the winkers. There was a
look of resigned despair on the man's face, but the steed had
dosed off.

'How much for an hour's hard riding?' I asked boldly,
trying to look the part of Attila the Hun, who had lived on
the back of a horse.

'Hold on', the man advised me. 'Better try him first. He's
temperamental, oo know. He might as well rusht and not
move a hoof off the ground he's shtandin on. Yerrah, sure
you can pay me after. We won't fall out about the priche.'

I sprang to the saddle and reached for the reins. 'Hold

on', shouted a photographer. 'That's a wonderful shot. I won't be a minute.' He clicked his shutter and collected three half-crowns. 'Three copies you want?' he asked. I nodded. 'Give me your address, sir, and I'll post them on. You'll have them by Tuesday.' He was as good as his word.

I adjusted the stirrups and asked for a whip. It was given to me.

'Gee up, old horse, gee up!' I commanded in my best cowboy accent and applied the whip. Nothing happened.

'Shir,' his owner suggested, 'maybe if you sthruck up a stave or two it would do the trick.'

'I've got spurs that gingle, gangle, gingle.'

As we both rode merrily along, I sang, but the steed never moved.

To say that I was embarrassed is putting it mildly. Don Quixote de la Mancha could always lower his visor if people mocked him, but I had no helmet to protect me. Moreover, his steed, Rocinante, did move. If only I had a Sancho Panza! His ass would be a means of escape from this ordeal. Old Doyle whooped with delight. 'My horshe he washe white although at first he was grey. He took great delight in travelling by night and by day. His deeds they were great if he could but the half of them tell. He washe rode in the Garden by Adam the day that he fell', he sang. 'Or whisper! Could he be the horshe of Troy by any chance?' The little knot of people who gathered round us were in stitches with laughter.

Doyle was not to be sneezed at. He had a good smattering of the lore and learning that came down from Owen Roe O'Sullivan and the mighty Aogán Ó Rathaille and he retained the great sagas of the past for recitation to an audience who could understand them. Why wouldn't he, in any case? Hadn't they the best and the most brilliant hedge-school masters in the kingdom of Kerry, and so the old learning lived and flourished there while it wilted and fell into decay in other parts.

Recently I called into Kate Kearney's cottage and inquired for Doyle.

'Who was he?' the assistant who was selling a thumping big *shillelagh* to a Yankee tourist asked me by way of reply. And going forth I wept bitterly, but not for the reason that Peter shed tears long ago.

The Fair of Puck I did not attend, for on the August bank holiday week-end I hoisted my sails and set a course for the land of Conal again. I had received a permanent post up there and as the hare whom hounds and horns pursue pants to the place from whence, at first, he flew ... and all that.

Bryan McMahon and Eamonn Kelly accompanied me as far as that watering-place called Bracing Bundoran that, according to Roddy the Rover of long ago, sets tourists all roarin'. They were outward bound for the holy island of Lough Derg not too far from Pettigo, but they were in no great hurry to pray and fast or run the gauntlet of Saint Brigid's bed.

And so we meandered through Clare, Galway, Mayo, Sligo and Leitrim to reach the fringes of Donegal three days after leaving the town of Listowel. The first night was spent at Lisdoonvarna in County Clare. There was an old friend of Bryan's stopping at the house of hospitality where we put up. She had a wonderful turn of phrase in both languages and recounted a most moving story about an experience she had had once in a remote part of the Connemara Gaeltacht.

She went to Sunday mass there and was struck by the air of sincere devotion manifested by the congregation. These people went to mass to pray and worship and not just to be seen, or because it was the custom to go. But she was not prepared for what was to come. At the consecration the people rose off their knees and surged forward towards the alter rails and, as the host was raised, stood with outstreched arms and chanted, '*Fáilte romhat A Thiarna Íosa Chríost!*' Her story touched us to the quick. Surely the faith moves mountains, and they were mountainy folk.

Saturday found us in the city of the tribes after a tour of the Burren country and a stop at Kinvara where Bryan insisted I sing *The Ol' Plaid Shawl* and *Galway Bay* in homage to Francis Fathy, that ardent lover of his native county. In Eyre Square we embraced the statue of Padraic O'Connaire and Eamonn Kelly and proclaimed Fred Higgin's lovely lament for Padraic O'Connaire. We visited the *Taibhearc,* tucked away in that narrow street next door to the quiet, candle-flickering Augustinian church where, I am happy to say, iconoclastic clerics have as yet made little headway.

As we proceeded on our conducted tour of the Gaelic theatre, the guide was loud in his praises of the pantomime they produced there the Christmas before.

'You should have been here to shee it, Mr McMahon', he enthused. 'It was evident that with this character Bryan was the salmon of knowledge on the ford above the weir bridge. Eamonn Kelly and myself were mere *harry pakeries* in that stretch of water. The *diabhal* himself was mighty. We had him up on a pedesticle and, at the appointed time, he disappeared in flames down to the bad place. You shee, he was standing on a trap-door and when the bolt was drawn he went down the chute. Shimple enough, of course, but very impresshive.'

We left him. 'Whatever you do for the rest of this day,' Eamonn Kelly beseeched Bryan, 'for God's sake keep us far from pedesticles. Barnum said there was one born every minute, but it was only because he had no second hand on his watch!' 'Easy Eamonn, easy man! We can't all be Solomons. And even he had his little frolics.'

'King Solomon, that monarch wise, had thrice three hundred lovers.'

'He had wives and queens and concubines, as the scripture it uncovers', I sang.

We left the guide on his pedesticle and made our way for the Great Southern Hotel where we dined in state. Bryan was greeted by umpteen American visitors dressed in outrageously coloured light suits and chewing the butts of massive cigars, but thankfully none of them asked us to sing *Danny Boy.*

At a singing session in a pub later that evening over in Dominic Street, *The Valley of Knockanure* did get an airing and a Spiddal man gave us a most delightful rendering of *An Droighnean Donn*.

On Sunday morning, after an early mass in the Augustinian church, we hit the road for Tuam where the last of the high kings of Ireland, Rory O'Connor, had reigned. After lunch in that town it was evident that McMahon was ill at ease, and as 3.30 p.m. approached he got steadily worse. A malady akin to that afflicting Riastradh Chuchulainn had overtaken him. The Sunday before, Kerry could only draw with Clare at a Tralee venue and the replay was fixed for Ennis on this very day. The sight of a wireless pole aggravated his condition. We had no watch, but there was a clock of sorts in my prefect car. It registered 3.25 p.m.

'Stop!' Bryan shouted. 'There's a wireless pole at that house.' I pulled up and we beelined for the open door.

'Come on in', the man of the house invited us. 'The game's about to start.' The whistle, the throw-in and Kerry were away like the wind. They clocked up three quick points without reply. Bryan began to breathe freely again. The palor left his cheeks and his eyeballs ceased rolling. Eamonn leant over to me, 'He's coming round. I think he'll make it.' I nodded discretely.

At half-time we thanked the people of the house for their hospitality and drove on to Milltown. At a crossroads outside the village there was a small group of middle-aged men throwing horeseshoes. Bryan asked me to pull up. He approached the most senior of them who was in the act of aiming his missile at the upright spud.

'Where can I find M J Molloy, the writer, around here?' he asked.

'It would take a shmart man to tell you that', came the reply.

'He lives over there in the bushes, but you won't get him at home of a Sunday.'

'And why?'

'He'll be away takin' shtatements off some man', he was told, and the tone, although caustic, managed to convey pity for a man who indulged in such antics. We pushed on.

Near the level-crossing at Ballindine another wireless pole stood straight and stout near about. Before I had switched off the ignition MacMahon was over the sod fence, down the garden and across the threshold. We stayed there listening to Michael O'Hehir roar himself hoarse until the second half ended. Kerry won at a canter and we continued our journey quietly. The fever left Bryan and after a snooze in the back seat he was as right as rain.

Towards twilight we reached Drumcliffe in County Sligo and made the *turas* to Yeats's grave. After the customary throwing of eyes at life and death we proceeded in the general direction of Bundoran. Near Bunduff bridge, on the Sligo-Leitrim border, I was lilting that lively old reel, *The Bird in the Bush*, with much degree of animation. Subsequently, MacMahon spread the rumour that I prevailed on the steering wheel to make the tires perform the intricate gyrations of the 'screwing' step with consequent peril to the passengers in the car. I assure you, dear reader, there was nothing of the crack.

I left the two Kerrymen discussing the future of this country in impeccable Irish with two Orangemen from Belfast at the bar of the Imperial Hotel, Bundoran, and headed home. My sister Annie, God rest her, was being married the next day.

5

Mac Reamoinn on the North-West Frontier

During the Lent of 1952 Sean Mac Reamoinn was touring the north-west frontier of Ireland, collecting songs, music and stories for *The Nine Counties of Ulster*, one of the finest people's programmes ever broadcast on Radio Eireann.

It was close to the soil, knowledgeable in relation to the crafts of that proud province and, above all, was faithful to the idiom of the people. Moreover, it spanned the political divide and was listened to by left-footers, right-footers and to that other race of people who never put a foot on a spade lug at all. Where would you find a pairing like Ben Kiely and Sean Mac Reamoinn within the four shores of Ireland or even across the herring pond in England's green and pleasant land?

Both broadcasters had their fingers on the pulse of the hidden Ireland and brought to their work that divine spark sadly absent from the pot-pourri folk programmes mashed up for us today.

Frank McKay, a county accountant with the Donegal County Council rang me one morning at 10.30 a.m. 'Take a day's leave', he commanded me, 'and repair to Lifford and Strabane where you'll find one Sean Mac Reamoinn of Radio Eireann waiting for you in the Imperial Hotel.' I needed no second bidding. The Ford was through the Keemy hills and past the white cross before Frank had time to change his mind.

When I reached the town of *Martha* and *Moorlough Mary*, Ned Nugent, the engineer, was recording Seamus O'Connor,

the county librarian, who was outlining the proposed stream-
lining of library services. Greetings were exchanged and
we got down to the nitty-gritty business of song recording.

Martha, the Flower of Sweet Strabane was the obvious choice
for a beginning and it was duly committed to tape.

THE FLOWER OF SWEET STRABANE
If I were king of Ireland and had all things at my will
I'd roam for recreation, and comforts I'd seek still
The comforts that I'd seek for, as you all may understand
Is to win the heart of Martha, the flower of sweet
    Strabane.

Her cheeks they were a rosy red and her eyes a lovely
    brown
And over her lily-white shoulders her golden locks fell
    down
She's one of the fairest creatures in the whole Milesian
    clan
And my heart is captivated by the flower of sweet
    Strabane.

I wish I had you, Martha, away down by Innishowen
Or in some lovely valley in the wild woods of Tyrone
I'd do my whole endeavour, and work the latest plan
For to win the heart of Martha, the flower of sweet
    Strabane.

But since I cannot win her love, no joy there is for me
I'm going to seek forgetfulness in a land across the sea
As down the Foyle the waters boil and the ship sails out
    from the lan'
I will say goodbye my darling girl, the flower of sweet
    Strabane.

Adieu unto the Foyle and Finn and the Mourne's
    waters wide

I'm sailing for America, no matter what betide
And since you will not come with me, I swear by my
   right hand
That McGilligan's face you will never see, Oh! flower of
   sweet Strabane.

Moorlough Mary is a remarkable song, carrying into
English the metrical structure of the poems and songs written
in the the eighteenth-century vision by poets practising in
the native tongue. There are as many stories about the fate
of Devine, the poet, who composed the song as there are
verses in it.

Moorlough is, in fact, a lake or lough away up in the
foothills of the Sperrins, not far from Donnymanna, that
supplies water to the town of Strabane. Now that gold
has been discovered in the mountain range, I do hope it
won't result in polluting that romantic stretch of water that,
to quote Ethna Carberry, 'lies in a world of heather'.

It seems that Mary Gormley or Moorlough Mary was no
great beauty at all. She was just a very middling-looking girl
with straight fair hair and pale blue eyes as an old shepherd
told me one evening in the June of 1953 when I was doing
research on the history of this famous lady. The work was
made much more congenial by the presence of a modern
Moorlough Mary with whom I was on very good terms at
the time. 'But,' as the shepherd commented, 'I suppose every
man thinks his own swan's the whitest.'

The poet Devine must have been familiar with the Gaelic
texts in which mention of Gormliath, the daughter of Flann,
one time king of Ireland, is made. The same Gormliath was
beautiful and was a poet of considerable standing. Moreover,
she had befriended many kings and high kings in their hours
of need. There is little doubt among the lions of learning that
Moorlough Mary's surname derived from the first name of
the poet-queen. Perhaps he saw in his own *spéirbhean* the
reflection of the first Gormliath.

Be this as it may, it appears he got a wee bit odd when she

denied him and quit going to mass on Sundays or attending weddings, *céilí*-houses or wakes, where there would be a bit of crack. Instead, he retired to a townland in the Lagan land of east Donegal to a place they call Black Repentance, and there pined away like the great Don Quixote de la Mancha:

> Sun, moon and stars from my sky you've taken
> And God as well, or I'm much mistaken.

It's tight when Cupid's arrow is driven home, they tell me. Whatever the fate of Devine, he gave to our traditional singing heritage one of its finest songs. Here it is:

MOORLOUGH MARY
The very first time I saw my Moorlough Mary
Was in the market of sweet Strabane
Her killing glances were so engaging
The hearts of young men she did pre-pan.
Her smiling glances bereft my senses
Of peace or comfort either night or day
And in silent slumber I start and murmur
'Oh! Moorlough Mary, won't you come away?

'Were I a man of great education
Or Erin's Isle at my own command
I would lay my head on your snowy bosom
In wedlock bands, love, we'd join our hands.
I would entertain you both night and morning
With robes I'd deck you both night and day
And with kisses sweet, love, I would embrace you
Oh! Moorlough Mary, won't you come away?'

If you had seen her on a summer's morning
When Flora's fragrance bedecked the lawn
Her neat deportment and manner courteous
Far, far surpassing the lamb and fawn.

On this I ponder where'er I wander
And thus grow fonder, sweet maid, of thee
With your matchless charm beyond comparin'
Oh! Moorlough Mary, won't you come away?

On Moorlough's banks now no more I'll wander
Where heifers graze on yon pleasant soil
Where lambkins sporting, fair maids resorting
The timorous hare and blue heather bell.
I would press my cheese while my wool's a'teasing
My ewes I'd milk by the break of day
While the whirring moorcock and lark allures me
Oh! Moorlough Mary, won't you come away?

Now I'll go down to my situation
My recreation is all in vain
On the River Mourne where the salmon's sporting
The rocks re-echoing my plaintive strain.
Where the thrush and blackbird do join harmonious
Their notes melodious on the river brae
And the little song birds do join in chorus
Oh! Moorlough Mary, won't you come away?

So farewell my charming young Moorlough Mary
Ten thousand times I bid thee adieu
While life remains in this glowing bosom
I'll never cease, love, to think of you.
Now I'll away to some lonely valley
With tears bewailing both night and day
In some silent arbour where none can hear me
Since Moorlough Mary, you won't come away.

Towards tea-time I happened to mention the Cuchuliann Céilí Band from Castlecaldwell in County Fermanagh and the fiddle players from that area. There was Phillip Breen of Ballygee, a noted performer, Eddie Moore from Corlea, one of the great old-style players, and, of course, the inimitable

Mick Hernon, who could shoot snipe and hook large trout almost as well as he could play traditional music.

'Isn't there a Joe Tunney down there somewhere too who plays a box? I have heard tell of him.' He looked me straight in the eye.

'There is, of course. He's a brother of mine, but I thought maybe you'd dislike nepotism.'

'He's your brother then?'

'Who else!'

'Well, that beats fighting cocks!' the grainy-voiced man with the winning smile exclaimed.

'And then, of course, there's Paul Coyle from Fassagh, I think it is, and Vincy Keown, the king's son from Killybig who plays tin whistle and piccolo, and I nearly forgot P J McGuire who plays the piano. The drummer is also a relation of mine.'

'How near?'

'Just a brother.'

'We'll go there', Mac Reamoinn said. 'Can you get word to them?'

'I'll try', I assured him, and went off to ring my brother Joe in Belleek. I was told to come on. A number of musicians would be alerted, he stated, but warned that although you could bring a horse to the water you couldn't make him drink. Some of them might be microphone-shy.

So we set out for Belleek over Scrathy Mountain but detoured a little to call on An t-Athair Peadar MacLoingsigh, the revered parish priest of Aughayarran, a pastor widely known and well respected in Irish language circles at the time.

The detour delayed our arrival considerably but this did not seem to dampen the enthusiasm of the large crowd assembled in Johnie McCabe's hall, whose only contribution to the recording would be applause, they well knew.

The hall was a tin structure and the acoustics did not measure up to the level of a recording studio, but, at the same time, when the band rattled off a medley of lively reels and jigs, and some of the soloists went through their paces, Sean Mac Reamoinn was satisfied that the game had been worth the candle.

And then he forced me to sing *The Enniskilling Dragoon*. It was not a song I was in the habit of singing, but, with heroic promptings from Johnie McCabe, I managed to get through it in a kind of a way. It's part of our tradition, so why not give it an airing?

THE ENNISKILLING DRAGOON
A beautiful damsel of fame and renown
A gentleman's daughter near Monaghan town
As she rode by the barrack, this wonderful maid
She stood up in her coach to see Dragoons on parade.

These Dragoons were all dressed just like gentlemen's
 sons
With their bright shining bayonets and their carabine
 guns
With their silver-mounted pistols, she observed them
 full soon
For they were royal, loyal Enniskilling Dragoons.

She looked on the brave sons of Mars on the right
With their armour outshining the stars of the night
Saying, 'Willie, dearest Willie, you have listed full soon
To serve as a Royal Enniskilling Dragoon.'

'Oh beautiful Flora, your pardon I crave
From this hour and forever I will be your slave
Your parents they have slighted you both morning and
 noon
All because that you love an Enniskilling Dragoon.'

'Oh Willie, dear Willie, don't mind what they say
For children must always their parents obey
But when you leave old Ireland they'll all change
 their tune
Saying the Lord may be with the Enniskilling Dragoon.'

Fare ye well Enniskillen, fare ye well for a while
And every blue border of Erin's green isle
When the war's all over we'll return in full bloom
And they'll all welcome home the Enniskilling Dragoon.

It was a memorable night. An RUC man at home on holidays approached me.

'Patrick, would Mr Mac Reamoinn be interested in *The Yellow Rose of Texas* or *Teddy McGrath*? Those are my favourite songs.'

He was anxious to record them for posterity, he stated, and I was in sympathy with his wishes. However, there were problems. While Sean Mac Reamoinn may not have met a yellow rose as yet, he was tormented with red roses. There was *The Rose of Mooncoin*, *The Rose of Aranmore* – 'That grand colleen, in the gown of green', *The Rose of Tralee*, and a whole hedge of Blarney roses. As far as I knew, Mr Mac Reamoinn, as the policeman called him, preferred his own little dark rose best. He styled her *Mo Róisín Dubh* in the native tongue.

I'm afraid he didn't exactly twig the cut of my gimp, but I had no time for further explanations. I assured him, however, that Radio Eireann would be most pleased to record *Teddy McGrath*, that good old anti-recruiting song, and the fact that it was sung by an RUC man would add spice and flavour to the performance.

The penny dropped.

'I don't think they'd like it at headquarters. A man might get into trouble over it', he mused.

'You know what's best for yourself, and far be it from me to encourage you to sing something to which your superiors might take offence.'

'Maybe we'd better leave it', he sighed. 'Still, I don't see why Mr Mac Reamoinn is so particular about the colours of his roses. "A rose by any other name is still a rose"', he quoted.

'Or by any other colour too', I hastened to add.

It was well after 2.00 a.m. next morning when Ned Nugent and Sean Mac Reamoinn climbed into the recording van and headed for the warmth and comfort of the Great Northern Hotel, Bundoran. They returned the next day and had interviews with spokesmen in world-renowned Belleek where Mac Reamoinn was put to the pin of his collar to weave words to match the intricate craftwork being made in the 'flowering shop'. That he succeeded is a measure of his ability as a broadcaster. Old men still speak of the night Radio Eireann came to McCabe's hall.

6

Omagh Town and
the Bards of Clanabogan

OMAGH TOWN AND THE BARDS OF CLANABOGAN
From sweet Dungannon to Ballyshannon
From Cullyhanna to Ol' Arboe
I've roamed and rambled, caroused and gambled
While songs do thunder an' whiskey flow.
Oh blithe an' airy I've tramped through Derry
An' to Portaferry in the County Down
But in all my rakin' an' merry-makin'
My heart was achin' for Omagh Town!

But life grew dreary an' I grown weary
Set sail for Englan' from Derry quay
An' when I landed the fates commanded
That I to London should make my way.
'Tis many a gay night from dark till daylight
I passed with people o' high renown
But in all the glamour and uproarious manner
My lips would stammer, 'Och, Omagh Town!'

Now further goin', my wild oats sowin'
To New York City I crossed the sea
Where congregations of rich relations
Upon the harbour did welcome me.
In fine apparel, like duke or earl
They soon arrayed me from sole to crown
But with all my grandeur and heaps to squander
My heart would wander to Omagh Town.

When life is over an' I shall hover
Above the gates where Saint Peter stan's
He'll kindly call me for to instal me
Among the saints in the golden lan's.
An' I shall answer, 'I'm sure it's gran', sir
To play a harp an' to wear a crown
But still, bein' humble, I'll never grumble
If Heaven's as charmin' as Omagh Town!'

High praise, indeed, for the town on the Strule, immortalised in prose by Benedict Kiely, the father of Irish letters, in this dark and violent twentieth century of ours. Ben, like myself, was under the impression this splendid song had been penned by one of the great Ulster poets of the eighteenth century in the direct line of the renowned William Carleton himself, but, as Sean O'Boyle the noted scholar and authority on traditional song and music once said, it is difficult to be certain about anything in Ulster.

The song is sometimes compared with Castlehyde, a song from the Blackwater district of Cork, which it resembles in verse construction and assonance, that was composed around the beginning of the last century. I give here a verse of the poetic effusion made by the mute, inglorious Milton from Blackwater side:

There are fine horses and stall-fed oxes, and dens for
   foxes to play and hide
Fine mares for breeding and foreign sheep there with
   snowy fleeces in Castlehyde
The grand improvements they would amuse you, the
   trees are drooping with fruit all kind
The bees perfuming the fields with music, which yields
   more beauty to Castlehyde.

It was not until September 1990 that I discovered that the author of *Omagh Town* was one Michael Hurl, who was a native of the Newbridge area of south Derry and the townland of Annahorish. His collection of verse and songs was published by the *Irish News* in November 1949. The title of the slim volume is *On Lough Neagh's Banks* and it contains forty-five poems and songs in all. Needless to say, *Omagh Town* is the one with greatest appeal for a traditional singer.

Little is known of the poet, for he lived most of his life in Luton near London where he was employed as a journalist.

It is interesting to learn that the Gaelic metre of the eighteenth-century *Aisling* poets has survived to be reflected in the poetry of Hurl, as late as 1949, even if he uses the borrowed Bearla.

Not far from Omagh town, on the road to Lack and near to the Minniburns, dwelt the Kearneys, a bardic family of rare distinction whose fame would be sung were I to remain silent.

There was Felix, or Faley, the father, whose song *The Hills Above Drumquin* is heard wherever Ulster singers gather to throw grace notes at the golden gates of heaven. It was my privilege to meet him in the old homestead in Clanabogan during the summer of 1951, and I must confess his son's lines in the lament he composed after his father's demise describe the man much better than I could ever hope to.

'Long and lithesome, cool and cheerful, strong and straight as any arrow.'

Felix wrote many songs and poems but his memory will live in the hearts of the people through his nostalgic *Hills Above Drumquin*, with its passionate love of place. Here it is:

THE HILLS ABOVE DRUMQUIN
God bless the hills of Donegal, I've heard their praises
   sung
In days long gone beyond recall, when I was very young
Then I would pray to see the day before life's race is
   run
When I could sing the praises of the hills above
   Drumquin.

I love the hills of Dooish, be they heather-clad or lea
The wooded glens of Cooel and the fort on Dun-na-ree
The green-clad slopes of Kirlish when they meet the
    setting sun
Descending in its glory on the hills above Drumquin.

Drumquin, you're not a city, but you're all the world to
    me
Your lot I will not pity should you never larger be
For I love you as I knew you when from school I used
    to run
On my homeward journey through you to the hills
    above Drumquin.

I have seen the Scottish Highlands, they have beauties
    wild and grand
I have journeyed in the Lowlands; 'tis a cold and
    cheerless land
But I always toiled content, for when the hard day's
    work was done
My heart went back at sunset to the hills above
    Drumquin.

When the whins across Drumbarley make the fields a
    yellow blaze
When the heather turns to purple on my native Dressog
    braes
When the sandstone rocks of Claramore are glistening in
    the sun
Then nature's at her grandest on the hills above
    Drumquin.

This world is sad and dreary and the tasks of it are sore
My feet are growing weary, I may never wander more
But I want to rest in Longfield when the sands of life are
    run
In the sheltering shade of Dooish and the hills above
    Drumquin.

Felix related a very good story of a night he spent being
entertained by neighbours in a local pub shortly after he had
composed this song. He had sung it for the umpteenth time
and many of his neighbours had gone home. Two Ederney
cattle smugglers arrived and gained admission, even though
it was past closing time. It was evident they had been doing
a pub crawl for they were already in a merry mood.

One of them started to sing *The Hills Above Drumquin*, but
although he had all the words his singing voice was not
of Caruso's calibre. When he finished, Felix added another
verse he composed on the spur of the moment. It ran:

> Drumquin, you're not a city; you're the town that God
>   forgot
> And the man who sang your praises was entitled to be
>   shot
> For the finest land in Longfield wouldn't grow a decent
>   whin
> And a goat would die with hunger on the hills above
>   Drumquin.

The Ederney men were incensed with rage. They wouldn't
stand idly by and listen to Felix Kearney being mocked. No!
In soul they would not. One of them drew an ashplant and
drove Felix out into the clouds of the night.

'That'll teach him to have manners and stop insulting the
Bard of Clanabogan! Who is he anyway?'

'That's Felix Kearney', the barman told him.

'Go to hell!' he exclaimed, 'You're codding me!'

'It's the God's truth', he was told.

Still he wasn't a bad devil, for he went the whole way to
Kearney's next day to apologise and gave Felix a robbery for
two wee stirks he had for sale.

Another of Felix's better known songs is *Dancing in Glenroan*. It evokes the lively atmosphere of the *céilí* house,

or rambling house if you like, where neighbours met to swap reel steps, tunes and songs or raise splanks from the flagstones with the crigging and clattering of hobnail pavers. I'm afraid this lovely old custom has nearly died out even in the remotest districts.

Hereunder I give the song and its translation into rich, flowing Gaelic by Felix's bardic son Arthur.

DANCING IN GLENROAN

By the turf fire brightly gleaming, I am sittin' idly
    dreaming
For 'tis pleasant to recall again the joys that we have
    known
And I find upon reflection that my fondest recollection
Is the fiddle's lilting music and the dancing in Glenroan.
Every jig and reel I mind them; in my memory I can find
    them
Bringing back the scenes of childhood and the joys that
    long have flown
Though I'm growing old and weary, still my heart is
    never dreary
When I dream the dream that brings me back the
dancing in Glenroan.

Sure the girls they were the sweetest and their dancing
    was the neatest
You wouldn't find their equal in the county of Tyrone
While the boys were strong and steady; you would
    always find them ready
With a *fáilte* for the stranger to the dancing in
    Glenroan.
And while sitting here I ponder, till my heart is filled
    with wonder
Why we ever leave such pleasure for a world so cold
    and lone
And I wish I were returning to begin again life's
    morning

But dreamland only brings me back the dancing in
   Glenroan.

Now, outside the snow is falling, evermore and more
   recalling
To my memory the long ago and joys that I have known
And my kindest thoughts are going with the breezes that
   are blowing
To drop the snowflakes gently on the hillsides of
   Glenroan.
And though time for me's advancing, don't I know
   there's youngsters dancing
In some cottage by the glenside where my thoughts
   tonight have flown
And that joy may aye betide them and the light of
   heaven guide them
For Ireland will be Irish while there's dancing in
   Glenroan.

It is a most moving little song, you'll agree, but listen to what
his son, who had the advantage of singing and speaking in
the native tongue, does with it!

RINNCEOIRI GHLEANN RUAIN

*I mo shuí annseo go seasgar damh, cois tine mhóna
   shlachtmha r*
*Bím ag cuimhniú ar an aimsir nuair ba ghaireach geal
   mo chroí*
'S nuair a smaoiním ar an aoibhneas a ba mhó a líon m' óige
Cluinim ceol a sheinnt ar fhidil agus trup na rinnceoirí.
Siar sna bliainta téid mo smaointí agus cluinim gar na daoine
Agus port acu a bhualadh agus ríl a scapfadh bron
Tá an aois anois 'mo chéasadh, ach ní leanmhar lom mo laethe
Nuair a cluinim ceol na fidle agus rinnceoirí Ghleann Ruain.

Mar ba deise na cailíní 's a rincíocht ba liomhtha na a
Bhfaca fós i ngleannta glasa grianmhara Thír Eoin
Cé gur stuamdha iad na fir, siad a d'fearadh fíor-chaoin fáilte

*Rolmh na cuairteoirí a thigeadh chughainn ar lorg sgeilp 's
ceol.*
*'S narbh amaideach gur bhreag mé nuair a bhog mé liom
as Éirinn*
Agus dfhag 'mo dhiaidh na daoine a ba dilse croí ar domhan
*'S nar dheas dá bhfeadfinn pilleadh siar ar duthchaigh bhreá
mo shinnsir*
Ach tré bhrionglóidigh amháin a tćim rinceoirí Ghleann Ruain.

Sneachta séidte ar na sleibhte, bheir mo cheann arís na laethe
Nuair a b'aoibhinn agam aisling 's ba dhóchosach mo chroí
*Agus sgaoilim siar mo bheannacht chuig mo mhuintir ins na
gleannta*
Ar gach feothan gaoith' a sgaipeas sneachta mhín ar fud na tír'.
Ta mo shaol-sa beagnach sceoidhte ach ta dream og lach, laidir
Teacht le chéile dtoigh a rince mar a rinneadh fad, fado
Gur ba sasta sáimh a saol-sa 's go seoldah Dia go deo iad
'S go mbuanaidh Sé an fidileoir agus rinceoirí Ghleann Ruain.

*Seacht m' anm duit A Airt! Tá feith na filíochta comh tréan,
laidir ionnat indiú agus a bhí ar an lá ud a thog tú mo chroí le
feadalaigh Fuiseog An tsleibhe i siopa na mbróg!*

Very often writers are at pains to convey the lack of
understanding between father and son. They attribute it
to the age gap, or to crabbed youth and age, and go on
inventing polite, meaningless terms to describe a condition
which does not exist outside their own feeble and imma-
ture imaginations. There is certainly no evidence of such a
condition in the relations between Arthur Kearney and the
quiet, civilised poet who was his father. Theirs was a case of
perfect understanding. Nowhere is this more striking than in
the son's tribute to his deceased poet-father. I give it here in
full with the consent of its author. It is not to be sung. Rather
it should be read and ruminated upon, for in it is revealed the
depth and tenderness of a son's love for a father who did not
fail to pass on his talents.

A Son's Tribute To His Poet-Father

Walk a little way with me back through eight and
eighty summers

Back through eight and eighty winters, walk a little way
with me

And we'll meet and talk with simple men and hear the
dying murmurs

Of a thousand lonely melodies, from Dooish to the sea.

See beyond the greening meadow in the shadow of the
hillside

Where the mountain stream comes leaping down through
hazel, heath and thorn

See the little, two-roomed cabin, roofless now and gone
to ruin

There begins my simple story, that's the place where he
was born.

There he spent his carefree childhood, close to nature,
close to hunger

Here he heard the skylark singing where the roots of
life begin

There he ran a barefoot schoolboy through the happy
haunts of summer

Snatching scraps of education in the school beside
Drumquin.

All too short the days of childhood, now he enters his
Golgotha,

Starts his *via dolorosa* through the farmlands of Tyrone

Long and lithesome, cool and cheerful, strong and straight
as any arrow

Penned his songs and laughed at hunger, found a wife
and built a home.

Come with me across to Scotland, where he found a
second homeland

Some strange magic in the Highlands filled a longing in
his soul

Then the blood-stained fields of Flanders, war and want
  and senseless slaughter
Wounded, weary, he came through it, back to Ireland
  and his goal.

Bear with me while we wander by the bridge across
  Glenfern
And we'll step aside a little and walk up the mountain
  lane
There it stands, bereft of bushes and the flowers that he
  planted
But I think his spirit bides there and I hear his voice
  again.

There he watched his children growing, sang them songs
  and told them stories
Cut the turf and swung his scythe among the fields of
  hay and corn
Always singing of the beauty of the rivers, glens and
  mountains
Of the simple things of nature in the land where he was
  born.

But the years go rolling onward and the eyes of one
  who loved him
Closed in death and left him lonely in the winter of
  his life
But he walked his road in silence, hid his sorrow from
  the stranger
Yet his eyes had lost their sparkle when he laid to rest
  his wife.

Walk with me a little further, for the journey's almost
  over
Demon death, the dark deceiver, took his stand beside
  the door
Sapped his strength and drained his life-blood, yet we
  never heard him moaning

But the vigour that had buoyed his soul was gone
   forevermore.

Walk in sorrow with me, slowly, let no clamour break
   the silence
Let no murmur mar the beauty of his passing from our
   ken
Walk beside me as we carry Felix Kearney from the
   alter
As the organ plays the last farewell, the mass *Rock in
   the Glen*.

Walk the last sad steps beside me, where the sun shines
   through the pine trees
As we lay the gentle poet down to take a mighty rest
There we leave him to his maker and the prayers of those
   who love him
Where the wild flowers of his native land are growing o'er
   his breast.

Nor can I leave the bardic Kearneys without reference to
young Felix, Arthur's brother. He does not use the quill to
communicate with us but writes his poetry with a fiddle
bow. Those of you who have had the good luck to have
heard him will bear me out when I say the old bard shared
his talents among his sons.

7

In Aughalea and Ol' Arboe

'It's pretty to be in Ballinderry, it's pretty to be in Aughalee', begins that lovely old lament called *Ballinderry*; and when the poet sat down to compose the incomparable song, *Ol' Arboe*, he invoked the gods and *na naoi mnaoi deasa* to aid and inspire him in his task.

We are in Lough Neagh country, the land of song and legend where even an inane character like Tom Moore thought he saw 'the round towers of other days in the waves beneath him shining', and attributed the 'vision' to a straying fisherman lest the sophisticated gentlemen who frequented the drawing-rooms of Dublin in his time would laugh him to scorn.

I asked Geordie Hanna if he ever saw these round towers shining in the waves beneath him when he was hauling in hundreds of eels, and he told me most solemnly, 'No, Paddy, I never saw round towers, but I hooked one eel bigger than the Lough Ness monster and it broke the stoutest hook on my line and sweeled itself in a couple of miles of my eel line! Boys, the size of that fish! He was a *tarrah!*'

And in Lough Neagh country were bred and born perhaps the two greatest traditional singers of east Ulster. I refer to the same Geordie Hanna of Derrytresk and Robert Cinnamond from Glenavy. Cinnamond came of weaver stock and, as is the tragedy in most cases, the collectors came too late. After his death, much of the precious material was either lost or forgotten. Notwithstanding this, it is incredible the number and variety of songs he still memorised and sang delightfully.

Perhaps the most notable of his vast store of songs is
Ballinderry, a song referred to by Bunting in his 1840 volume,
The Ancient Music of Ireland, as the finest example of a tune
in which the chorus, or *crónán*, is almost in perfect harmony
with the melody.

That the great collector of the old harp music should think
so highly of this tune and song to print a version of it in
his 1840 volume is not to be wondered at when we hear
the song sung by Robert Cinnamond. Here it is, as I recall
it being sung by the famous Glenavy troubadour.

BALLINDERRY
It's pretty to be in Ballinderry
It's pretty to be at the Cash of Toome
It's prettier to be in bonnie Ram's Island
Trysting under the skies of June.

Crónán: Ochon! ochon! ochon! onchon!

It's pretty to be in little Ram's Island
And side by side with Felimy, lover
And he would whistle and I would sing
And we would make the whole island ring.

Crónán

It's pretty to be in Ballinderry
It's pretty to be in Aughalee
And he would court me, though I be coy
At heart I loved him, my gentle boy.

Crónán

'Twas pretty to be in little Ram's Island
But now it's sad as sad can be
For the ship that sailed with Felimy, lover
Is sunk forever beneath the sea.

Crónán

And oh, that I were the weeping willow
To wander alone by the lonesome billow
And cry to him over the cruel sea
'Oh, Felimy, lover, come back to me.'

Crónán

This form of song or lament is perhaps the best example of keening, or *caoineadh*, present in the English language. That it is derived from the Irish, there is not the slightest doubt. A most highly developed and sophisticated form of crying after the dead existed in Gaelic-speaking Ireland for centuries and had a degree of professionalism about it. Indeed, it could bear some affinity to the official mourning carried out at funeral services even at the time of Christ.

I only heard it once on an off-shore island and it seemed to me a very faint echo of the heart cry in Máire Áine Nic Donncha's *Úna Bhan*, or the soul-harrowing sorrow conveyed to listeners when Seosamh O h-Eanaigh sang *Amhran na Páise*. What a shame if this genuine form of the *caoineadh*, exemplified by those two magnificent *sean-nos* singers, were allowed to die out!

Another famous song in the repertoire of Robert Cinnamond is the one associated with our great poet W B Yeats. It is *The Rambling Boys of Pleasure*, first heard by the poet from an old woman who sang it as she sat milking her cow in a field outside the village of Ballisadare in County Sligo. The poet listened patiently to her singing and then went off and penned his famous poem, but he had the courtesy to subtitle it, *An Old Song Resung*.

Lesser poets turning the secret joinery of song have borrowed or stolen from songs in the idiom of the people without any apology to the mute, inglorious Milton who often wove the original verses.

I have been listening to songs and collecting them for a goodly number of years and I must say that Cinnamond's version of *The Rambling Boys*, and another sung by Tim Hastings over in Westport in County Mayo, are the only versions of this beautiful song I have ever heard.

Here now is Cinnamond's version of that rare and racy song:

THE RAMBLING BOYS OF PLEASURE

You rambling boys of pleasure, give ear unto these
   words I write
For I own I am a rover and in rambling I take great
   delight
I have set my heart on a handsome girl, though often
   times she does me slight
But my mind is never easy, only when my darling is in
   my sight.

Down by yon flowery garden, where me and my true
   love do meet
I took her in my arms and to her I gave kisses sweet
She bade me take life easy, just as the leaves fall from
   yon tree
But I being young and foolish, with my own true
   love could not agree.

The second time I saw my love, I vowed her heart
   was surely mine
But as the weather changes, my darling girl she changed
   her mind
Gold is the root of evil, the more it wears a glittering
   hue
Causes many a lad and lass to part, though their hearts
   like mine be e'er so true.

I wish I was in America, and my true love along with
   me

Money in our pockets to keep us in good company
Liquor to be plenty, a flowing bowl on every side
Hard fortune ne'er could daunt me, for we are young
   and the world is wide.

Over in Derrytresk, on the west bank of Lough Neagh,
reigned the Conor MacNessa of Ulster singers, the mighty
Geordie Hanna. No need for me to sing the praises of this
wonderful singer. He would be praised if I kept my silence.
Geordie was not moulded in tradition; he was quarried out
of it. Next to my mother, Brigid Tunney, God rest her, he
gives me more listening pleasure than any other traditional
singer I have ever heard.

His style is a sincere, honest one that appeals to the
heart. Hence there is no need to strain after effect. It is,
of course, a highly personalised style that defied imitation.
Hence, my advice to young singers who are straining their
vocal chords to sing like Geordie is not to attempt it. You'll
only throttle yourselves. By all means learn his songs, but
sing them your own way. His was a gift that was only
given once.

Here is one of his most moving exile songs. Listen to the
master:

WHERE THE GREEN SHAMROCK GROWS
Farewell my native Irish home, my friends both one
   and all
My luck lies in America, let it either rise or fall
From my cabin I'm evicted and now compelled to go
And leave this sainted island where the green shamrock
   grows.

I owed the landlord two years rent, I wish I owed him
   more
That day the sleeky bailiff he put a notice on our door
My wearied, widowed mother it grieved her for to go

And leave the house my father built some fifty years
    ago.

She lingered for a little while; she fretted and she died
The only consolation that she sleeps by father's side
I'll pray for them both night and day wherever I may go
Till I return to Ireland, where the green shamrock
    grows.

Farewell to my acquaintance, with whom I used to sport
At the youthful dance on a Sunday where colleens do
    resort
There's one I leave behind me, it grieves me for to go
And leave her in old Ireland where the green shamrock
    grows.

But with youth and vigour on my side, and in the best
    of health
And fortune only favours me, I'll be a man of wealth
And when I've saved some money, it's back to her I go
And we'll live together happily where the green shamrock
    grows.

Now the good ship lies at anchor, the tender's in the bay
To take on board the passengers going to America
With a bunch of blooming shamrocks Saint Patrick bless
    of yore
Saying, 'You're welcome to America when you're from
    old Ireland's shore.'

So hurrah my boys! The sails are hoist; the wind is
    blowing fair
Full sail for Castlegarden; in a few days we'll be there
It's hard to leave the ones you loved and in your heart
    you know
And leave the sainted island where the green shamrock
    grows.

And on that western shore of the big lough on a rise
at Arboe Point stands a monumental high cross generally

referred to as the Old Cross of Arboe. It dates back to the tenth century A.D., and so it would seem that if Saint Patrick ordered it to be 'raised on high', the people of Tyrone took their time in obeying his command.

The ruins of a sixteenth-century church and the remnants of a small, ancient building still called Arboe Abbey are close by. The older ruins may be part of the early monastery of Arboe but little is known about it. It is associated with Saint Colman Mucaidhe, who is said to have founded it towards the end of the sixth century.

A local legend relating to the building of this monastery by Saint Colman would appear to account for the name *ard bó*, or cow's height.

They say that as soon as the masons began work a miraculous cow came out of the lough, and not only did she supply the builders with sufficient milk to drink but also with enough to slake the mortar being used. Hence it was that they had no need to go searching for ox blood with which most of the mortar was mixed at the time. When the abbey was completed, the cow returned to the lough and neither hilt nor hair of her has been seen since.

Still, Geordie always maintained that her progeny are still to be found in the area, which accounts for the high yield of milk from Arboe cows down to this very day. Isn't it a *tarrah*!

The cross fell in the early nineteenth century or, some say, was pulled down at an earlier date by iconoclastic Cromwellians, and indeed there is a very bitter poem in the Irish language where the cross invokes a curse on those responsible 'for the pulling down of me'.

It is a masterpiece of invective and demonstrates what a fine language Gaelic is for praying, love-making or cursing.

It has been raised again, and to date no one has had the temerity to interfere with it. Here now is Geordie's splendid song, *Ol' Arboe*.

OL' ARBOE

Ye gods assist my poor, wearied notion, ye inspired
    muses, lend me your hand
To exert my quill, without blot or blemish, till I sing the
    praises of this lovely land
That's well situated in the north of old Ireland; being all
    in the county of yon sweet Tyrone
Joining the banks of Lough Neagh's bright waters, is
    that ancient fabric they call Ol' Arboe.

I stood in amazement to view the harbour, where purling
    streams they do gently flow
Where the trout and salmon they were nimbly sporting;
    which brings more wonder to you, Ol' Arboe
In the summer season for recreation you can carelessly
    stray along those strands
Where Borea's breezes are gently blowing along the spot
    where the fabric stands.

It was Saint Patrick who did adorn that great stone cross
    sure he placed on high
That each spectator would well remember that on a cross
    God's son did die
I have travelled Russy and parts of Prussy, I have
    travelled Spain and beyond the Rhine
But in all my raking and undertaking, Arboe, your
    equal I ne'er could see.

'I got that song off Dan McCann', Geordie went on to say.
'Dan was a grand man. Boys, he had some great spakes!'

Geordie had the gift of fashioning the idiom of the people
into rich poetry. Some of his comments leap live at you from
the anvil of the muses.

He built a large bungalow to accommodate his good wife
and twelve children. Some begrudging neighbour suggested
to him that a smaller house would have done, but Geordie
silenced him for all time.

'What do you mane?' he asked him. 'In the last house we were crowded just like frogs in a *sheugh*!'

On another occasion he returned triumphantly from a *fleadh cheoil* where his singing had been greatly enjoyed by the attending multitudes.

'Boys, oh, boys!' he told his family, 'it was a pity you missed it. When Hanna or another singer, who shall be unnamed, was singing you could hear a flea scratching himself! Isn't it a *tarrah*?'

On another occasion he came home from one of the big singing gatherings in the Carleton Hotel Belleek where it was his luck to share a room with a troubadour who had scanty regard for soap and water. 'Boys, oh boys, you should have seen him when he took off the shoes and socks! You could have sowed leeks between his toes!' he declared.

Geordie Hanna, you may be gone from us but wherever Ulster men gather together to raise their voices in song you will be in our midst. If Seamus MacMathuna and Brian O'Rourke and 'big' singers from the other provinces join our circle, you will be the first to find a welcome spot for them near to the hearth and our hearts. May the green sod of Ireland lie lightly on your bones!

Now Geordie had many sisters and brothers, but the one known the length and breadth of this country, and indeed beyond it, is Sarah Ann O'Neill, for she can wind a song with the best of us. Her repertoire is inexhaustible and her variety of songs incredible. Space will only permit one sample to be given here, but it is one that will wet the appetite for more. Her great song is *Dobbin's Flowery Vale*. Usually performers sing only four verses of the *Vale*, but Sarah Ann does not believe in half-carts. I give you here the entire eight-verse version sung to Sarah Ann's own air. There are at least two other airs to this renowned Armagh song.

Alas! the *Flowery Vale* is now pock-marked by a housing estate and you are unlikely to find lovers by the river side there any longer.

DOBBIN'S FLOWERY VALE

One morning fair as Phoebus bright her radiant smile
   displayed
As Flora in her fragrant garb the verdant plains arrayed
As I did rove throughout each grove, no cares did me
   assail
When a pair I spied by the river-side in Dobbin's
   flowery vale.

As I sat down them to behold beneath a spreading tree
The limpid stream that gently rolled conveyed these
   words to me
'Farewell, sweet maid', the youth he said, 'for now I
   must set sail
And bid adieu to Armagh and you and Dobbin's
   flowery vale.'

'Forebear those thoughts and cruel words that wound a
   bleeding heart
For is it true that we're met here, alas, so soon to part
Must I alone here sigh and moan to none my grief
   revale
But here lament my cause to vent, in Dobbin's flowery
   vale.

'There's many a youth has left his home to steer for
   freedom's shore
Been laid beneath the silent tomb where the foaming
   billows roar
Take my advice, do not forsake or leave me to bewail
But still remain with your fond dame in Dobbin's
   flowery vale.'

'Unwilling am I to part with you, no longer can I stay
For love and freedom cry "pursue", these words I must
   obey
In foreign isles where freedom smiles or by the earth
   concealed

I will come home, no more to roam from Dobbin's
   flowery vale.'

'It's when you reach Columbia's shore, some pretty
   maids you'll see
You'll never think on the loving vow that you have
   made to me
May hope content life's ending pain! My heart would oft
   prevail
Of seeing no more the youth I adore in Dobbin's flowery
   vale.'

'Do not reflect that you're alone, nor yet am I untrue
If e'er I chance far, far to roam my thoughts will be
   on you
There's not a flower in shady bower, on verdant hill or
   dale
But will me remind of the maid behind in Dobbin's
   flowery vale.'

Then mutual love together drew them in a fond embrace
While tears like gentle drops of dew did trickle down
   her face
She strove in vain him to detain, but while she did
   bewail
He bade adieu and I withdrew from Dobbin's flowery
   vale.

8

I Would I Were in Monaghan

'You'll come to the *fleadh cheoil*, Joe', I coaxed my brother on the morning of Whitsunday, 1 June 1952.

'Damn it, I don't know, Paddy', he replied. 'We have Irvinestown to play in the championship this evening. There's a *feis* on there and they want a late throw-in.'

'Never saw them a day better. Always looking for favours. How late is late?'

'Half-seven', he told me. 'Still, if we win and I have a leg to stand on, we'll go.'

He was as good as his word. The Belleek Young Emmets won and Joe and our younger brother Michael returned with their shields. With Irvinestown well beaten and the turf clamped we could afford to enjoy ourselves at the All-Ireland *Fleadh Cheoil* in Monaghan Town on Whit Monday.

We headed away for Monaghan around 10.00 p.m. The sun was setting red and fiery away out over Bundoran and only the high ridge of Toura rose above the shadows. It was nearly midnight when we reached our destination to find a *céilí* in full swing. I mind well we had two Donegal tweed suits at the time, but we were not long dancing until the jackets had to come off.

Two of the Coyle girls from Fossagh had preceded us to the *fleadh* so we danced them until well into Monday morning. When the *céilí* ended we escorted them to their granny's house past hissing ganders and the hags of the night.

We were early a' foot next morning, for Joe had entered the accordion competition, and so we withdrew some distance out the Clones Road and Joe had a last run over the tunes he proposed to play in the contest. There was a fair in

Monaghan that day too, for marts were unknown at the time and men driving herds of bullocks and heifers before them stopped to flake out a few steps to *The Pigeon on the Gate* or *The Sligo Maid.*

Joe did well enough in the contest. He tied for second place and was recorded by Sean MacReamonn. Vincent Broderick won the flute competition and MacReamonn made me hold down Vincent's foot so that the strong beat on the floor of the recording car would not drown out the rounded notes of flute music. The year before, when *Comhaltas Ceoltoiri Éireann* was launched in Mullingar at *Feis Lar na h-Éireann,* Paddy Kelly of Bundoran carried off the coveted fiddle prize. However, Clare was well to the fore in Monaghan and the great Bobby Casey emerged as champion fiddler for that year. I can still hear his wonderfully traditional version of *My Love's in America,* and that's thirty-nine years ago.

Highlights of that *fleadh* were the playing of Sean McGuire and Leo Rowsome at the concert. Eamon OMurchaidhe, from Tydavnet, was the moving spirit of the *fleadh* and he sang a lovely little song about a fiddle that wanted its owner to take it into the bed as it was cold on the wall. I wonder, have any of our song collectors succeeded in rescuing that song for posterity?

There were no song or lilting competitions held by *Comhaltas* that year and it was not until the following year that traditional singing was taken seriously enough to warrant the setting up of a competition. That year there was a mighty thunder-storm during the Sunday night concert. Lights went out and candles had to be fetched and lighted, but the musicians played away. Lightning flashed in forks and tongues of flame. The audience could be forgiven for thinking that the Holy Spirit was descending on the traditional musicians of Ireland.

In 1954 the *fleadh cheoil* moved to Cavan and singing and lilting competitions were included. I won the first lilting championship there that year and successfully defended my title for the next two years in Loughrea and Ennis respectively, and then, like my namesake Gene Tunney in the boxing world, decided to retire undefeated. I didn't want the embarrassment of a long count.

Whatever criticism is made of *Comhaltas Ceoltóirí Éireann*, it cannot be denied that the organisation came about when Irish traditional music and song were broken and bleeding and that they have been restored to their rightful place in our heritage largely by the efforts of that organisation. *Go mairidh sé beo na céadta bliain*! I got married in 1955 and myself and my good wife, Sheila, headed off for the All-Ireland *Fleadh Cheoil* in Loughrea, County Galway on the Saturday afternoon. In those days when honest toil was taken seriously, public health officials worked a half-day on Saturday. Charlie Roche, first children's dental officer to be appointed in Donegal, got a lift with us as far as the Skeffington Hotel in Eyre Square, Galway.

We were to have picked up Tomas O'Duibhir near the Star of the Sea Church in Bundoran, but as I was slightly late in arriving there, Tomas had accepted a lift from a small cattle-dealer who was carrying two bullock stirks in the back of his van. The same locomotive had seen better days and the springing was not the best. And so, when the livestock spaltered and dunted about in the back, the rusty little vehicle lurched and canted all over the road. At one time, Tomas thought it was beginning to waltz, but as there was no music audible he put the curious feeling down to a colourful imagination. Moreover, he was wearing his best suit of clothes, and accidents can happen with bullock stirks. Although we have made rapid strides in public health we have yet to teach our bovines how to use flush toilets or even pail closets.

Tomas was glad to part with his cattle dealer in Ballisadare and we picked him up on the straight stretch of road going into Coolooney. All went well on the road to Galway and mighty and profound were the philosophical discussions Charlie Roche and Tomas indulged in. Then, as we left Eyre Square and headed for the Dublin Road, didn't the ring gear on the starter stick. We were directed to an off-duty mechanic who released the jammed mechanism in a couple of seconds and charged me a pound note for his pains.

In Oranmore in County Galway we put up that night on a bed as hard as the rock flag that supported Diarmuid and Grainne when they fled the wrath of Fionn MacCumhaill.

It was a most enjoyable *fleadh*. Everyone was there. Sean 'Ac Donnacha, Willie Clancy, Sean MacReamonn, Ciaran MacMathuna, Paddy Canny and the entire Tullagh Céilí Band, the Seerys and Leo Rowsome.

There was a certain unaffected gaiety, a spontaneous friendliness about those early *fleadhanna* that seems absent at such festivals today. Perhaps success tarnishes the spirit of movements that spring naturally from the hearts and souls of the people.

The Ennis *Fleadh Cheoil* held in 1956 was memorable for me more by events that took place on the return journey than by the functions at the *fleadh* itself. Michael, my younger brother, and the legendary Mick Hernon, noted fiddle-player, angler and sportsman from far-famed Derrarona, accompanied me on the long trek to the capital of the banner county.

It was Sunday night when we reached Ennis and there was no room at the inn, or indeed anywhere else within the precincts. Kevin Vaughan, the efficient *fleadh* secretary, arranged accommodation for us out at Ennistymon in the Falls Hotel and we were very comfortable there. When the main events were over the *fleadh* began in earnest so that it was Wednesday afternoon before we were dragged away from Clare. In fact, Michael was so impressed that he was talking of leaving the banks of the Erne and heading for the Cliffs of Moher. His lengthy exposure to the hidden Ireland nearly turned his head. At length, head prevailed over heart and equilibrium was restored.

When we reached the outskirts of Tuam, Mick Hernon was so tortured by a reel he had half-learned at the *fleadh* that he asked me to stop. He took out his fiddle and finally cornered and captured his tune at the little crossroads between Tuam

proper and the Belclare-Caherlistrane road. There was a turf
bank close by and four hefty men were breast-sleaning and
barrowing turf there.

So spirited was Mick's playing that my brother and myself
could no longer relax on the soft grass of the roadside
but leaped out on to the tarmac and began to dance a
big, wild reel. The turfmen stuck their spades and came
running. When we finished they applauded with whoops
and handclapping.

It was then their turn to treat us to a Galway half-set, and
I wish you'd have seen yon boyos flaking and battering away
with abandon, their wellington tops turned down. There is
no gainsaying it. Contentment is wealth and the Galway
turf-cutters had it in abundance.

That was the *fleadh* that inspired Robbie McMahon to
write his brilliant and witty *Fleadh Cheoil In Ennis*, and at
which he first sang, in his own inimitable style, the rousing
song *Spancill Hill*. Mrs Mulcaire's singing was in full bloom
round those years and indeed her *Lovely Willie* almost became
a vogue song.

I did not get to Dungarven in 1957. A baby was being born
to us every year and certain domestic chores had to be seen
to, but I well remember the Whit Monday of that year. I was
clamping turf up in Barnes Gap, but all the day I fancied I
could hear the echo of reels on the breeze that blew steadily
from the South.

The next year brought us the Longford *Fleadh Cheoil* which
was, in my opinion, one of the best ever held. A new star
arose in the firmament of traditional singing in the person of
Josephine MacNamara, the linnet from Aughavass who took
the country by storm. She was one of the sweetest singers of
our best traditional songs. I believe she is living in the States
now. Brightness of brightness I met on the desert way . . .

9

Francy Curran: King Of Killymassney

'Francy Curran, they say, has a rake of good songs', I probed old Johnie Callaghan of Cark one evening when I was paying him for a turf bank he had lent me. As he handed me back the half-crown luck-penny, he gave me the assurance I sought so eagerly.

'Lord man, do you see, when Big Francy was at himself forty or fifty years ago he could sing more songs in one night than you'd shake a stick at!'

'Is he hard to coax?' I went on to ask.

'I wouldn't think so. But when he does start you'll have a job stoppin' him. He couldn't have whistled me a better tune.'

A fortnight later, Bill Harney from the Northern Territories of Australia came to Dublin looking for songmen, as he called them. Invariably, he went to Radio Eireann, which was housed in the attic of the GPO at the time. Sean MacReamonn pointed him in my direction and in time he arrived at Labbadish in the lap of the Lagan where I was then living. The house belonged to Billy Patterson and was known as Green Cottage. There was a fine, big bawn in front where I grew sufficient vegetables and potatoes for ourselves, and Billy had advised my wife, Sheila, to get a dozen or so pullets to dispose of the surplus grain that was going to loss in the farmyard to the rear of the dwelling.

Access to the house was gained through the farmyard gate, but there was also a little side gate that opened on the road and a narrow path that led directly to the front door. Only the foolhardy or the uninitiated ventured to approach by this route as it was guarded by clumps of savage nettles more deadly in combat than a battalion of fiery dragons.

Bill Harney was too familiar with the briars and brambles of the creeks in the Northern Territories to fall into the clutches of Lagan nettles, but other visitors to Green Cottage were not so fortunate.

The man from the creeks down under had lived and worked with the Aborigines and boasted loudly of the manner in which he took young crocodiles and all species of fish, and so I resolved to show him a way of fishing about which he knew nothing.

And so this June evening of sunshine and showers we set off for Lough Dale and I parked the car on Francy Curran's street. As we approached the lough, a light smur of rain began to fall and a south-west breeze freshened. I used the otter-board, or dolphin as they call it in the Toura country, with a cast of a dozen flies. There was a good take and I was catching the trout in sixes and sevens at a time.

'Golly, Paddy, I never saw anything like it', Bill exclaimed. 'Why, you're stringing them like nappies on a clothesline!'

In no time at all we had two bags of nice trout and headed back for the car. It's a good two miles of rough terrain from the shores of Lough Dale to the Curran household and Bill Harney, for all his boasting about trekking in the bush, wasn't used to the rough knowes and whitehole *curraghs* of Ballygallen Mountain. Consequently, our progress was slow. Besides, we were weighed down with two heavy bags of trout. So between the jigs and the reels it was dusk when we made it back to the wee byre at Curran's gable.

We sat down on a rocky flag to draw our breath and Bill began asking about songs. Up from the lean lands of Lennalay a linnet note reached our ears, and out on the bogs of Ballygallen a moorcock screathed softly. The scene was set. I began to sing *The Mountain Streams Where the Moorcocks Crow* and looking up I could just make out the tall figure of a man standing still but upright near the little gate. It was the old monarch himself and he was listening intently. I finished the song and we went towards him.

'Did ye's kill many trouts?' he inquired as he held the gate open to let us pass through, and then, 'What is the name of that song you were singing? Boys, oh boys! It has a lovely air! But what are we standing here for? Come on away in. Ye's must be hungry as hawks.'

We needed no second bidding but followed him over the threshold. There was tea made and eggs boiled and the sweetest and yellowest country butter I ever saw or tasted laid before us with lashings and leavings of home-made bread baked in a pot oven with live coals heaped on the lid. It was a meal fit for a king. I wouldn't let the *bean an tí*, Francy's daughter-in-law, light the Tilly lamp, for the glow of the black turf *greeshagh* was much more in keeping with the occasion.

We sat there and swapped songs until the early hours of the morning. The Australian left with his head reeling. In truth, it had been a bardic night.

So when Ciaran MacMathuna came on one of his rare visits to the north-west shortly afterwards, I landed him in Killymassney with Big Francy Curran, the monarch of the mountain:

> The mountain marrow braced his bone
> Hard granite set in monarch mould
> His tongue untethered silver tone
> Of sweetest sound, well veined with gold.

It is no secret that I used Big Francy as the man and the singer in my poem *The Man of Songs*.

I mind well the Friday afternoon when Ciaran, Ned Nugent and myself arrived in Killymassney with Francy Curran. Willie, his son and Willie's wife were away in Letterkenny shopping when we got there, but still the man himself gave us a hearty welcome.

No time was lost in setting up recording equipment. Ned

sat at his post in the recording van, 150 yards down the trail from the house, and the microphone was mounted on the hearthstone. Francy Curran began to sing. His first song was named *Henry and His Maryanne*. I give it hereunder.

HENRY AND HIS MARYANNE
Come all you loyal lovers, a tale I will unfold
Concerning a young maiden fair and her young
    sailor bold
As they discoursed with each other, young Maryanne
    did say,
'Oh, stay at home, dear Henry, and do not go away.

'You will leave me broken-hearted, your absence to
    bewail
To think how you'll be tossed about by every winding
    gale
I'll forsake my friends and parents all, I'll dress just
    like a man
With you I'll go and face the foe, your own dear
    Maryanne.'

'Oh no, my faithful Maryanne, with that I'll not agree
For you to leave your parents dear and go along with
    me
Perhaps on board of a man-o'-war, our love it would
    divide
Oh, when some anchored cannon ball would stretch you
    by my side.'

'Then go, you faithful sailer lad, my heart still bleeds for
    you
May providence protect you every danger you come
    through
Do your duty manfully; may fortune guide your han'
Come back and wed your faithful girl, your own dear
    Maryanne.'

Going sailing on the ocean, far from our homes did steer

Some thinking on their own sweethearts, some others
   on parents dear
When every boy unto his girl does drink a flowing can
'Hurrah, my boys!' young Henry cried, 'Here's a health
   to my Maryanne.'

We sailed the stormy ocean for three long years and
   more
At length we got an order to sail for Erin's shore
The captain gave us fifty pounds the day we reached
   the lan'
That very day young Henry got wed to his Maryanne.

There is one song from this locality that every singer worth
his salt sings, be he good, bad or middling, and Francy
was one of the best. It is, of course, *The Hill of Glenswilly*,
composed by one Mick McGinley of Breenagh, Glenswilly,
on an outward bound voyage to New Zealand. It is a song of
exile and never fails to draw tears from Donegal folk far from
home. I recall singing it once in South Orange, New Jersey,
and there wasn't a dry eye in that packed audience.

Mick mailed the song home as soon as he landed, but he
didn't overstay his welcome down under. The postal service
was worse then than it is now and he was back 'among the
sycamores' of that grand old glen before the song arrived, or
so the story is told.

In my opinion, the long trip was well worth the song and
few glensmen would disagree with me. Francy Curran called
it *The Hills of Glensúilí* and of course he is right. *Gleann Súilí* is
the Gaelic way of spelling it, and Francy Curran had no time
for *cat breacs* or soup-suppers who corrupted or anglicised the
correct spelling of the far-famed glen.

THE HILLS OF GLENSÚILÍ
Attention pay, my countrymen, and hear my native
   muse
Although my song is sorrowful I hope you'll me excuse

I left my native country a foreign land to see
I bade adieu to Donegal, likewise to Glensúilí.

Brave, stalwart men around me stood, my comrades
    loyal and true
And as I grasped each well-known hand to bid my
    last adieu
I said, 'My fellow countrymen, I hope you'll soon be
    free
To raise the sunburst proudly o'er the hills of Glensúilí.'

Cursed be those tyrannical laws that bind our native
    land
Must Irishmen remain as slaves while we in exile stand
Brave countrymen who struck one blow to banish
    tryanny
When Leitrim's lord fell like a dog not far from
    Glensúilí.

No more among the sycamore I'll hear the blackbird
    sing
No more I'll hear the blithe cuckoo that welcomes back
    the spring
No more I'll till your fertile fields, a *chuisle geal mo
    chroidh*
On a foreign soil I'm doomed to toil, far, far from
    Glensúilí.

No more at balls or harvest-homes my violin I'll play
No more I'll dance the Irish jig among the girls so gay
My loving harp I've left behind, 'twill make them think
    on me
And keep my place till I return to lovely Glensúilí.

The summer sun was sinking fast beyond yon
    mountains grey
As I left lovely Glensúilí to wander far away
And as I glimpsed those grand old glens that were so
    dear to me

I thought my heart would surely break for leaving
Glensúilí.

Adieu to you, dark Donegal, my own, my native land
In dreams I often see your hills and towering mountains
grand
Alas! ten thousand miles do lie between your hills
and me
A poor, forlorn exile cast, far, far from Glensúilí.

May peace and plenty reign supreme along Lough Súilí's
shore
May discord never enter our Irish homes no more
And may the time soon come around when I'll return
to thee
And live as my forefathers lived and die in Glensúilí.

Aye, bás in Éireann! Isn't it the fervent wish and prayer of
every exile who left the sainted soil since Saint Colmcille
sailed down the Foyle many, many years ago? And to their
eternal shame, native governments are driving the cream of
our race away again!

Francy continued to sing. At one time, Curran's pony that
was running loose in the small fields surrounding the house
trotted in on to the street. The clop of his hooves is still
audible on the tape that was being made of the singer,
for Ciaran thought it would be a sin to delete it in such
circumstances.

Then Francy sung us the complete version of a rare song
seldom heard in Ireland, although Kennedy infers in his
Folk Songs of Britain and Ireland that it must have originated in
Ireland by reason of the fact that the young damsel's dwelling
was by the banks of the Shannon.

It has been collected in Sussex, Shropshire, Dorset, Hamp-
shire, and Oxfordshire in England and in Nova Scotia and
Newfoundland in Canada. In Ireland it was collected by
Colm O'Lochlainn and Sam Henry. It is known by various
names, such as *Her Serving Man, The Young Serving Man, The*

Daughter in the Dungeon, Love Laughs at Locksmiths, Since Love Can Enter an Iron Door, and *The Cruel Father*.

Where did Francy Curran, shepherd and songster who was never further from his native heath than Strabane in County Tyrone, get this song? The only conclusion I can come to is that he got it off a broadsheet at a rabble day in Letterkenny or Raphoe. These were the old hiring fairs where the planter farmers of the Lagan hired the sons and daughters of the native Irish in those infamous slave markets.

I give hereunder the text of Francy's version and the tune he used. (Francy's version does not allude to Shannon Banks or to the lofty mountain, but mention is made of Ireland. He calls his song just plain *Mary Ann*.)

MARY ANN
I'll sing of a damsel who's tall and handsome
Her former beauty to describe I can
And every fellow belonged to nature
She fell in love with her servant man.
Her hair was black as a raven's feather
Her form and features to describe I can
There was a young man worked on the station
She fell in love with that servant man.

As young Mary Ann and her love were walking
Her father saw them and nigh them drew
As young Mary Ann and her love were talking
Her father home then in anger flew.
He swore an oath much too vile to mention
To part these lovers he's contrived a plan
To build a dungeon with breek and mortar
Full fifty fathom all underground.

The food he gave her was bread and water
The crudest chair that was for her he found
Three times a day he did cruelly beat her
And left her weeping there underground.
Three times a day he cruelly beat her

Till to her father she thus began
Saying, 'If I've disgraced you, oh honoured father
I'll live and die for my servant man.'

When young Edward found out her habitation
It was close confined by an iron door
He vowed in spite of all the nation
He'd gain her freedom, or rest no more.
So at his leisure he toiled with pleasure
With aching back and a blistered han'
Full fifty fathoms he dug to the basement
To secure release for his Mary Ann.

He dressed his love then in men's apparel
To put his sweetheart all in disguise
Saying, 'I'll stay here and I'll face your father
When he sees me it will him surprise.'
When her father came with the bread and water
It was for his daughter he loud did roar
'I'm her', said Edward, 'I've freed your daughter
For lover can enter through an iron door.'

When he saw Edward all in the dungeon
It was like a lion he loud did roar
Saying, 'Out of Ireland I'll have you banished
Or with my broadsword I'll spill your gore.'
'Come use your pleasure and without measure
Come use your pleasure, do all you can
For it's at my leisure, I'll die with pleasure
To secure release for Mary Ann.'

When he saw love so strong that could not be parted
He fell on his knees on the dungeon floor
When he saw love strong and so tender hearted
He broke the chains of the iron door.
Young Mary Ann and her love got married
They roll in riches just as they can
Young Mary Ann, she is blessed forever
She cries, 'My faithful young servant man.'

Francy sang many other songs, mostly of the land war and of agrarian strife or of parochial struggles between the Blue Shirts and Fianna Fail, but, as some of them have been known to raise the hackles on local political zealots, I think it is best to let sleeping dogs lie.

We left Francy Curran in all his glory high up in the hills of Killymassney with the scent of heather honey and the crow of moorcocks to keep him company. Some years later he was called to God and now sleeps in a graveyard on the banks of the Swilly near historic Scarriffhollis where the Gael made a last stand against the Cromwellian hordes. The great voice is stilled forever, but his songs live on.

10

'Twas Fate Commanded

'You're for seeing her I believe', big Michael ribbed my brother Joe as they sat at their benches in the flowering shop of the world-famed Belleek pottery, making the renowned baskets on a dark day just before Hallowe'en.

'Seeing who?' the little man asked.

'The Queen, of course', big Michael replied with special emphasis, but he did not raise his voice. Quiet-spoken, dignified men never need do so.

'Damn, but it could lead to fame and fortune!' chimed in James Mulrone. 'Wasn't it a chance meeting with some big shot in London town gave Charlie Chaplin his first break?'

So the cat was out of the bag. Duffy, the local news mole, had delved deeply and the tidings were splashed across the pages of the *Donegal Democrat* that week-end, proclaiming to Ireland and the world that Joe Tunney, of the famous Cuchuliann Céilí Band and flying winger on the Young Emmets Gaelic Football Team, would perform at an international folk concert in the Royal Festival Hall, London, on 7 November 1958. He would be accompanied by his brother Paddy.

Joe was never a man for publicity, but why hide one's light under a bushel? Much better to let it shine before men, I always held. True, Duffy's caption had upstaged me. Ah the hell, what odds! 'For I being humble will never grumble if heaven's as fair as sweet Mulleek town!'

The tickets arrived: first-class travel by boat and train from Belfast City to London and ten pence per mile to the Farset Mouth and back. It was not to be sneezed at. The English Folk-Dance and Song Society were sorry their funds could not afford air travel, but they assured us we'd be comfortable enough. We were.

In London we were put up in folksy houses. Our hosts were well-heeled professionals who had embraced abstract socialism. They talked endlessly about marathon marches they had taken part in. One firebrand had actually sustained a blistered toe in his exertions to ban the bomb!

I was cross-examined about the bother in the North which at that time manifested itself only in gerrymandering.

'Gracious goodness! I have read a whole book on the subject', my *bean an tí* informed me, 'an authentic one too, recommended by the *New Statesman*, and do you know, Paddy – do you mind if I call you Paddy? You can call me Beatrice – I am still very much at sea in relation to the problem.'

I advised her not to be discouraged. I had lived there most of my natural life and I was still grappling with the problem. I was quizzed about James Joyce, Bernard Shaw and James Connolly. Did I think Brendan Behan was a great writer? And what of his contribution to the folk-song revival? When I sang her *The Ol' Triangle* she declared she was thrilled to the marrow.

Came the concert on the afternoon of the seventh. A mighty host of entertainers had been assembled, I must admit. When called upon I sang *The Mountain Streams Where the Moorcocks Crow* and *Lough Erne Shore*. Joe followed with *The Sligo Maid* and *The Boys of the Forty-Five*, the only reel Seamus Ennis didn't know. Then, with the connivance of Peter Kennedy, I began lilting Maggie Pickins. Joe took up the tune and our sister Bridie floated out on stage and danced the twenty-four steps of that old Ulster folk-dance. To state that she stole our thunder would be putting it mildly.

Seamus Ennis followed and gave one of his finest stage performances in song, story and music. Bardic it was by any manner of measurement.

When the concert was over we were joined by Joe Heaney and the irrepressible Margaret Barry. The fare was rich and racy but when the circle widened to include Hamish Mor

Henderson and Jeannie Robinson and the Copper Brothers the spree went on till the small hours.

We stayed in London for a week or so and did recordings for the Cecil Sharp Library. It was during one of these recording sessions I had the singularly good fortune to meet Paul Robeson, surely one of the world's greatest blues singers. He was in Cecil Sharp House rehearsing a show for BBC television, and I met him in the corridor on the way to the gents. Peter Kennedy, who was hovering around, introduced us. When we had exchanged the usual polite, meaningless words I made bold to ask for a song. He courteously consented.

'What would it be?'

'*Old Man River*, please.'

He obliged. Never have I heard a song sung with so much soul and effortless artistry. When the applause died down he asked me to sing. There was only one song befitting such a rare occasion, and I sang it. It was *The Mountain Streams Where the Moorcocks Crow*.

He shut his big, sad eyes and listened intently. 'Ah!' he barely whispered, 'Fine, fine! But then you're Irish, of course.' The big man from the Mississippi and the wee man from the mountain streams gripped hands again, but never a word was uttered. For me it was an unforgettable experience.

11

In the Shade of Maeve's Cairn

It was *fleadh* time in Sligo. Paddy Killoran was home on holidays from the States and a great hosting of traditional musicians, dancers and singers thronged into that town to enjoy the music of the fiddling maestro from Ballymote.

From the province of Munster and the county of Clare came Willie Clancy and Sean Reid. Donegal sent Francie Kelly and Vincent Campbell. The home county fielded Joe O'Dowd, Fred Finn, Peter Horan, Willie Coleman, Johnie Henry and Seamus Tansey. Fermanagh was represented by a quartet of Tunneys: my mother, my sister Bridie, my brother Joe and myself. In fact, it was the only *fleadh* my mother attended.

I can clearly recall Willie Clancy's excitement when he learned she was present. When I went into a room in Kelly's Hotel overlooking the Garavogue River he ceased playing, discarded his pipes and hurried over to me.

'In the name of God, Paddy, where is she?' he exploded.

'Where is who?' I asked, pretending not to know.

'Your mother, you hoor!' he replied, 'Who else?'

'She went upstairs to the ladies', I informed him.

'Come on. Bring me to her.'

What could I do, only lead the way upstairs. As soon as she emerged from the bathroom he seized her in his strong arms and proceeded to hug and kiss her. My mother was visibly shaken. We Northerners are not given to such physical demonstrations of esteem, but when I assured her that it was Willie Clancy, the minstrel from Clare, and that he was a great admirer of her songs and singing style, she asked for a drink of water and, on request, sang him *The Mountain Streams* as Brigid Tunney only could.

It was a big moment for both of them. I wonder, do they meet in the halls of heaven; does she sing him that lovely old song, or does he play her favourite slow air, *Mo Buachaillín Bán*!

Competitions and such trivialities were dealt with efficiently and with admirable promptitude, and the crowds surged into the Gilhooley Hall for the big concert.

Paddy Killoran was of course the star performer and he played *Tansey's Favourite* and *The Heathery Breezes* with a spirit and abandon that matched his recorded reel playing of the thirties. *The Sligo Maid* with its compulsive urge to dancers to get up and shake their feet followed, but it was his rendition of that rare and romantic old jig, *The Geese in the Bog*, that captured the imagination of the audience.

He was requested to play it over and over again and it effectively upstaged *The Humours of Lisadell* and *The Maids of Castlebar* on that bardic night.

There were other great performances in the sphere of fiddle music at that concert given by Joe O'Dowd and Fred Finn while Clancy cast a spell on us all with his great piping and whistling. Seamus Tansey dipped his wooden flute in spring-well water and a cascade of wild and wonder notes fell on our listening ears, but it was Paddy Killoran's music we came to hear and he gave of himself unstintingly:

We will drink and be merry all grief to refrain
For we may or may never all meet here again.

How prophetic is the couplet of that old drinking song! Many or most of them are gone to God and only fond memory brings the light and laughter of other days to those of us left in the valley of tears.

12

From the Clear, Winding Ayr
to the Banks of the Tweed

My mother did not believe in casting pearls before swine nor in teaching her songs to singers incapable of singing them. She went in mortal dread of the day when some bawling balladeer might hobble on to a stage and, leaning heavily on his guitar crutch, proceed to mutilate and finally murder one of her favourite songs for the delectation of a mob of howling hoodlums, such as those who recently raped Croke Park.

Would to God that the rest of us had had her wisdom. We would be spared the indignity of hearing some of our best songs being tortured and savaged almost daily. Singing terrorists should never be suffered gladly.

Hence it was that there were certain songs she was loathe to let even her favourite son learn. One of these was *Burns and His Highland Mary*, or *The Clear, Winding Ayr* as it is called here in Ireland.

I recall a quiet, sunny Sunday evening in September 1966, just two days before my father departed this mortal world. Sheila, my wife, was chatting to him in the room and I was exercising all my powers of persuasion and diplomacy to extract the last verse of this song from my mother. My father smiled. 'He's going to get the last verse of that song from her this evening after twenty years trying', he chuckled.

The following year I was on a whistle stop tour of the folk-singing clubs in Scotland. My base was in Glasgow where I stopped with Geordie McIntyre and his wife, Maureen. When I was leaving they presented me with Ford's *Vagabond Songs and Ballads of Scotland*, and there I found a complete version of the song. The words tallied with my mother's version, but whereas Ford uses a short melody to match a four-lined verse, my mother sang a long, highly ornamented tune and telescoped every two verses together to form a long, eight-lined verse that suited her style of singing admirably.

It was not Robbie Burns who composed this song, of course. Some say it was composed by an unknown Glasgow policeman, but Ford does not mention him. He writes, 'No song touching the life of Robert Burns and his idealised *Highland Mary* — not one of the poet's own, perhaps — has found more favour with the country people of Scotland than this rhapsody of unknown authorship which had been widely circulated in broad-sheet form. Ballad-hawkers, indeed, still find it a "catch" at country markets and fairs.'

Here, now, is that magnificent song:

THE CLEAR, WINDING AYR, *OR* BURNS AND HIS HIGHLAND MARY
In green Caledonia there ne'er were two lovers
So enraptured and happy in each other's arms
As Burns, the sweet bard, and his dear Highland Mary
And fondly and sweetly he sang of her charms.
And long will his song so enchanting and bonnie
Be heard with delight on his own native plains
And long will the name of his dear Highland Mary
Be sacred to love in his heart-melting strains.

Oh, it was a May day and the flowers of the summer
Were blooming in wildness, all lovely and fair
When our two lovers met in a grove of green bowers
Which grew on the banks of the clear winding Ayr.
And oh, to them both 'twas a meeting full tender
As it was the last for a while they could hae
So in love's purest raptures they feasted together
Till the red setting sun showed the close of the day.

'Oh, Mary, dear Mary', exclaimed her fond lover,
'You carry my heart to the Highlands with thee

Every burn, every grove, every bank and green bower
May talk of the love of my lassie and me.
My life's sweetest treasure, my own charming Mary
To thee I'll be ever devoted and true
For the heart that is beating so hard in this bosom
Is a heart that can never love any but you.

'Oh, dinna bide long in the Highlands, my Mary
Oh, dinna bide long in the the Highlands from me
For I love thee sincerely, I love thee o'er dearly
To be happy so far, my dear Mary, from thee.'
'I winna bide long, my dear lad, in the Highlands
I canna bide long, for you winna be there
Altho' I have friends I love well in the Highlands
The one I love best's on the clear, winding Ayr.'

Then he kissed her fond lips that were redder than roses
And strained her lily-white breast to his heart
And his tears fell like dew-drops at e'en on her bosom
And she said, 'My fond lover, alas! we must part.'
'Then farewell', he cried and he flew from his Mary
'Oh, farewell', said Mary, she could say nae mair
Oh, little they kenned they had parted forever
When they parted that night on the clear, winding Ayr.

Yet the green summer saw but a few sunny mornings
Till she, in the bloom of her beauty and pride
Was laid in the grave like a bonnie young flower
In cold Greenock Kirkyard, on the banks of the Clyde.
And Burns, the sweet bard of his own Caledonia
Lamented his Mary in many a sad strain
And sore did he weep for his dear Highland lassie
And ne'er did his heart love so deeply again.

Then bring me the lilies and bring me the roses
And bring me the daisies that grow in the dale
And bring me the dew of the mild summer's evening
And bring me the breath of the sweet-scented gale.

Oh, bring me the sigh of a fond lover's bosom
And bring me the tear of a fond lover's eye
And I'll pour them all down on thy grave, Highland
    Mary
For the sake of thy Burns who so dearly loved thee.

My mother had another Scotch song she reserved for the long, bright evenings in July when men were melting barrels of bluestone on the headlands of potato fields to spray the healthy stalks that were beginning to meet across furrows, protecting them from the dreaded blight. It was a haunting song, full of the sound of nature and innocent love. Here it is:

THE BANKS OF THE TWEED
By murmuring streams all alone do I rove
How happy am I when I am with my love
He plays on his flute so delightful and gay
If he knew how I loved him, no longer he'd play.

No blackbird or linnet have ever sung so sweet
As I and my true love, when together we meet
The thrush and the skylark, they stop and take heed
As we sing to the groves on the banks of the Tweed.

I went into hiding beneath a green shade
To hear the soft plaint of an innocent maid
She flew to his arms saying, 'Willie, my dear,
Since you proved so inconstant, pray what brought
    you here?'

'Oh, Mary, forgive me in the grove all alone
It was not my intention to stay from you so long
I've come to visit my ewe-lambs and see my flocks feed
And to walk with you, Mary, on the banks of the
    Tweed.

'To the alter of Hymen straight we'll repair
I own that I love you, I vow and declare

We'll join hearts and hands while our lambs they go
    feed
And in wedlock we'll bind by the banks of the Tweed.'

It was on a Sunday morning that Geordie McIntyre and I
left Glasgow and set out on the long journey by motorway
for the granite city of Aberdeen. We were received by Arthur
Argo and his good wife, and after a hearty meal our host
offered us a choice of entertainment.

'We can go round to wee Jimmie MacBeth and hear some
of his randy stories or visit Jeannie Robinson and hear a
few of her best songs.' We opted for Jeannie and were not
disappointed.

Jeannie was in her element that evening and proceeded to
tell me that she had seen me on the bars of the grate when
the coal fire was dying down the evening before. Well I knew
she was a *spae*-woman who had also the power of cursing.
I recalled Norman Kennedy telling a story of himself and
Jeannie being storm-stead on a lonely road somewhere near
Blairgowrie one wild winter night.

They knocked at a farmhouse door and asked permission
to stay until the storm blew itself out.

'No, ye canna stay', the farmer had said, 'We have little
enough heat for ourselves.'

'Before a week of Sundays you'll have your fill of heat',
Jeannie warned him, but his mind was made up. They trudged
on and eventually found shelter in an isolated hay barn
where they slept cosily until morning. Seven weeks after, the
surly farmer who denied them shelter was burned to a cinder
in a freak fire that broke out in his own cowshed. Cattle were
also lost. The newspapers were at pains to discover the cause
of the fire. Norman Kennedy had no need to ask. The curse
of Jeannie Robinson had overtaken the farmer.

The story reminded me of two Aranmore men who were
cutting and clearing bracken off an upland farm in Fifeshire.
Their store of provisions was running short, so they made
their way to the farmer for whom they were working and

asked for cheese. He pressed his own, it seems. He refused their request. 'Very well', said the older of the two, '*Bas síóga lá gaoithe ar bhárr phíce!*'

They left. The next morning the lady of the house sent for them. 'Here,' she said, 'take all the cheese you want. My Willie died last night in his bed. I was gettin' fed up with him anyhow. He was very "near", ye know. Wouldn't even let me get in the electricity or anything. Ye did a fine job. Could you teach me that curse?'

But to get back to Jeannie Robinson and what she saw in the dying embers on the grate bars:

'I saw a friend, and he was coming from the west. Someone said you were coming to Scotland, Paddy. So I knew it could only be you.' Deduction goes hand in hand with divining, it seems.

We chatted for a while and then the singing session started. With very little coaxing she gave us one of the greatest of the big Scottish ballads, *Rolling in the Dew Makes the Milkmaid Fair*, in which she rolled her 'r's with a richness and a relish far beyond the range of any other traditional singer I have ever heard, and a version of *The Carle he Came Over the Craft* that would warm the cockles of Hamish Mor Henderson's heart. She ended with an earthy version of *Killacrankie* that none of us have encountered before or since. God rest you, Jeannie! Your singing heritage was a priceless one indeed.

The King is Dead!

It was a sultry day in June. There was a *feis* in Buncrans and my third son Michael, then just five years old, was entered in the elocution contest which was to commence at 5.30 in the afternoon. There were some urgent planning applications to be dealt with in the Twin town area of the county, so I headed away bright and early in the morning.

My last call would be with a Mr H Gillespie of an address somewhere near Ballybofey, and he proposed to erect a dwelling in the townland of Carrickmagrath. Could it be the king himself I'd be calling on? Could I ever be so lucky?

However, since the name Gillespie in the Sessiaghoneil parish is akin to McLaughlin in the peninsula of Innishowen, I could not be sure. True, I had seen in a local newspaper that the monarch of musicians was back on his native heath, but could I have such singular good luck as to meet him so soon?

I inquired in a house on the Corgary Road. 'Would it be the Yankee you're looking for?' I was asked in that subtle, oblique way people use to worm information from officials in rural Ireland.

'It could be', I told him non-committally.

'Try the two-storey house on the right, about a mile up the road. You'll see plenty of hens and ducks on the street and around the outhouses', he told me.

I followed his directions and arrived at the house. The door was open, but still I knocked.

'Come on in', a voice commanded me. It had the suggestion of an American drawl. My heart missed a beat. I was as lucky as a cut-cat!

'I'm looking for a Mr H Gillespie', I told the gentleman sitting at the fire. 'Does he stay here?'

'He sure does. I'm the man.'

'You have an application in for permission to build a house. Could we see the site?'

'Sure, sure!' he replied. 'We'll go right up now.' And that's how I met Hughie Gillespie, the king of fiddle-players and the finest performer on that instrument since the reign of Michael Coleman. We went to the site and I did what I had to do. A fine one it was, too, with a sweeping view out over the Finn Valley, and when I left him back again I was invited in for tea.

'And you're Hughie Gillespie, the powerful fiddle-player who made records with Coleman away back before the war?'

'What's left of him', he chuckled. After the tea I ventured to ask if he'd play a few tunes.

'Sure, sure,' he agreed, 'as soon as Rosemary comes back. Where did she take herself off to?' he inquired of his mother.

'She took a wee dander up the road but she'll be back shortly', he was told. And so she was. Rosemary, his daughter, was also a good fiddle-player and together they made a fine duet.

They had been playing at Father Flannagan's *aeriocht* the previous Sunday and the instruments were tuned a little higher than concert pitch for outdoor playing, and so it took a little while to readjust them. Then they began. In five minutes I was under the spell of the great Gillespie and clean forgot that I had to transport Michael to the Buncrana *Feis*.

Between the jigs and the reels it was 4.00 p.m. before I glanced at my watch. 'Great God, I'll be murdered!' I exclaimed. 'I am supposed to have my son in Buncrana for a *feis* competition that starts at 5.00 p.m.!'

I had to return to Letterkenny, pick him up and head like the hammers of hell for Buncrana, a round journey of forty-two miles, and I wasn't driving a Jaguar or a Rolls Royce.

Michael was waiting, all dickie-bowed up and on the verge of tears. My wife, Sheila, was not in the best of twist either. I got my son into the car and we dashed for the Innishowen capital. Going down the Slab Road I was travelling at sixty miles an hour and looking back occasionally to correct the words of his recitation. When we got to our destination there were only two more competitors to be heard.

The test piece in this particular elocution contest related to a mouse that had a terrible cold in its head and the devil himself couldn't stop him from sneezing. Michael was awarded second prize and brought the first medal into the household. I was quite proud of him, but my wife did not share my glee.

'Had the wee fellow got a proper chance and been driven at a normal pace to the *feis*, he'd have got first prize and no bother', she declared. 'But then, of course, you had to be away chaw-hawing through the country', she concluded bitterly. I sang dumb. You can't argue with a woman.

In the fullness of time the king of fiddle-players built his castle on that hill in Carrickmagrath and within ten years it was speared round by Sitka spruce and ringed with purple rhododendrons. It became the mecca of music lovers and fiddle-players until Hughie's lamented death at Hallowe'en in 1986.

In New York, Hughie Gillespie and Michael Coleman were loved, revered and respected. This fact was brought home to me forcibly when I toured the United States with the Irish group, brought out by the Smithsonian Institute, Washington, during the bi-centenary celebrations of 1976.

Wherever we went and whenever we were introduced to connoiseurs of Irish traditional culture and music, the conversation invariably centred on the genius of Gillespie and Coleman. 'Ah, professors Gillespie and Coleman!' they would exclaim. 'We shall never hear their like again! Those men were inspired.'

When one considers that they raised Irish traditional music

from the morass of mediocrity, into which it had fallen, and remoulded and refined it into a medium of expression second only to the Irish language, is it any wonder that they will be remembered forever in that great land of the free?

We in Ireland are, by and large, a nation of begrudgers. Talent is smothered, but genius is hissed at and hated. Is this attitude indiginous, adapted from our neighbours across the *sheugh*, or merely a manifestation of the herd instinct?

My meeting with Hughie Gillespie evoked memories of the excitement generated in west Fermanagh in the late thirties when word reached us that another record of Coleman or Gillespie was about to be released. Money was scarce at the time, but most music lovers would gladly have gone without breakfast to scrape and save the price of that precious disc.

I recall a fair in Belleek at the time of the cattle-smuggling. A well-known, widowed cattle-dealing woman entered Ross's, then the largest shop in the village.

'Great God Almighty, Mr Ross!' she shouted to the proprietor at the loud of her head, 'Have you got Lord Gordon?' Mr Ross was an ex-soldier who had fought with distinction in the Great War. He wore plus-fours mostly and went about his business with a brusque, military, off-putting air. It was plain that he was at sixes and sevens, but replied that he had never met the noble peer.

At that very moment Francy 'Bell' Keown, a lively and loveable troubadour who hawked the old seventy-eight speed records down the highways and the byways of the Loughshore country, came to the rescue and explained that it was a gramophone record by that name which the good lady wished to purchase.

I mind well the first time I heard Coleman's recording of *Lord Gordon's Reel*. It was nightfalling and I was out on the rocks, a heathery hump of high ground that looked down on Lough Erne, throwing an armful of hay to a couple of hungry stirks.

Maureen, my eldest sister, had come home from work triumphantly bearing with her the famous record. Lamplight spilled out over the half-door and with it came music. It was a calm, quiet, frosty night and down the air that was taut as a fiddle-string music drifted melodiously.

I stood there glued to the ground, bewildered and be-witched. Were the 'wee people' making this music? There was a fairy fort on the rocks that I knew well. Maybe the *sluagh sidhe* were abroad, but it was a calm night and they needed high winds or maybe a gale to mount the air. So I was safe enough.

Then it dawned on me where the music was coming from and I made a beeline back to the house.

When, at a later stage, I was discussing the spell cast on me by Coleman's great reel with John Cowan, unquestionably Fermanagh's finest all-time fiddler, the big man from the bar of Wheealt warned me, 'Paddy, man, you'll have to be fierce careful. Wait till you hear Master Crowley's reels or *The Star of Munster* played by Hughie Gillespie. You'll be whisked away to another world entirely and could get it tight enough to make it back!' How right he was. Munster musicians are indebted to the great Gillespie for putting a jewel in the crown of their star that outshines even O'Rathaille's *Brightness of Brightness*.

Hughie Gillespie was born near Ballybofey on 11 September 1906. His father played the fiddle, but he always maintained it was his uncle Johnie, reckoned to be one of the best fiddlers of his time, who made the deepest impression on him.

When he grew to man's estate and eventually began work-ing as a lumberjack on a local demesne, he *céilíed* around the rural districts with a neighbour of his own age named McGinley. They were working together and went to an odd sheep fair to deal in hardy little Scotch ewes. They were strong, strapping lads, full of the zest for life that gives youth its indefatigable energy. They frequented house dances together and courted girls in the same townlands.

This night they headed away for a dance and a raffle

in a house across the River Mourne in Aughayarn country.

As they crossed the mountains and marshlands, a thick mist came down suddenly and in the clapping of your hands the two boyos couldn't see a finger before them. Both men knew well there was a 'stray' on this stretch of mountain. It wasn't long until they knew they were clean a *shaughran*, but not a word passed between them.

Then Hughie thought he heard music. It grew louder and louder. It was fiddle music and the most haunting reel tune he had ever heard. A curious thing was that McGinley heard no music at all. Then, of course, he wasn't a fiddler.

They caught a glimpse of a light in the distance and made a beeline for it. No sooner had they started out on this new track than a smooth, moss-lined path like a carpet formed beneath their feet, but no matter how quickly they travelled the light seemed the same length away.

A fearsome sweat broke out on McGinley's brow. 'Christ, man,' he exclaimed, 'we're finished. We're on the Fairy Pass!'

They stood still, made the sign of the cross, took off their jackets, turned them inside out and put them on again that way. The mist dispelled as fast as it had come down and they found themselves standing on the *bruagh*, or bank, of a large white hole, or *scrath luinge*. Another step and the quagmire would have swallowed them like quicksand! It was a near thing indeed.

They quickly retraced their steps, thanking God for a timely deliverance, and had no difficulty in finding the raffle house some hundred yards up the slope.

'Had we gone on and slipped into the swamp', Hughie declared, 'we'd have been with the "wee people" still, and I'd have known every reel and rann in the whole universe!' Instead, they were happy to settle for the raffle house where a hearty welcome awaited them.

They were brought up to a mighty limekiln of a fire that blazed away on an open hearth, and in no time at all there was a steam rising out of their wet clothes like the reek from a still-house when you'd be running a 'heating' of poteen. The *bean an tí* made them take off their boots and socks, and she wrung the water out of the socks over red *greeshagh* near the hob and then hung them to dry on the arm of the crane crook.

While the hose and footwear were drying out, she brought them two mugs of steaming, hot tea and a couple of slices of wholesome home-made bread, buried in layers of sweet country butter.

The raffle was over but the patrons consented to a reshake of the dice, and didn't McGinley win the prize: a pair of ladies shoes with toes like toothpicks. He bestowed them on a wee girl he left past the gander that night, for if he had taken them home, he maintained, his mother would have banished him to his sad destiny, as the song says.

The music wasn't great: one scratchy fiddler sawing away and the hairs flying out of the bow, and two old women accompanying him on combs, but the dancers were enjoying themselves as they swirled through lancers, quadrilles, Highland flings, polkas, shoe-the-donkeys, stacks of barley, green-grows-the-rushes-oh, and big wild mountain reels.

The fiddler was in a lather of sweat, like a horse you'd ride too roughly over hurdles, not comparing the brute beast to the bullock stirk, as old Pat Gormley used to say in that delightful manner he had of mixing metaphors. Then, some one said, 'Young Gillespie plays the fiddle. He'll give you a break, Billy.'

The fiddle was reached to Hughie while Billy relaxed and put a leaf in the pipe. Until then he had only three tunes: *A Poor Man's Work is Never Done*, *The Keelero* and *Off She Goes With her Leg in a Pot*; but as soon as he caught the fiddle and retuned her, he was able to flake out hornpipes, Highlands, polkas, reels and jigs the like of which was never heard before or has been since.

The dancers were bewitched. They swirled and birled and battered out steps on the flag floor until clear daylight in the morning.

'It was the fairies were playing', Hughie declared afterwards. 'I was merely going through the motions!'

> Oppressive laws have stained the cause of many a boy
>   like me
> Our land's too small to serve us all, we had to cross the
>   sea
> For our green shore is rich with ore kept back by
>   England's crown
> And each green field, abundant yield, dear lovely old
>   Fintown.

And so Hughie, like many another worthy son of this green island, crossed the Western ocean to the land of the free. He took ship from Derry on 4 February 1928. On arrival in New York he went to stay with an uncle. Upstairs lived one Neil Smith who played bones in a band headed by Packie Dolin. Smith had a couple of records made by the mighty Michael Coleman, and on hearing them Hughie became anxious to meet their maker.

This was arranged and Hughie was thrilled when the maestro asked him to play. Coleman listened attentively. 'Very good!' he commented, 'But from this day forth you will be my pupil.'

In the years that followed a brotherly bond of friendship and mutual understanding was forged between them that was never broken.

Together they played traditional music, vetted tunes, improved and embellished them and salvaged for us a priceless part of our unique musical heritage. They also composed new tunes.

Hughie's normal work with Consolidated Edison, which in those days in New York would have corresponded with our Electricity Supply Board, did not preclude him from daily broadcasts on local radio stations with the Sligo maestro. These programmes were generally listed as *The Irish Hour* and were sponsored by business firms. The time was divided between advertisements and music. The two fiddle-players performed without accompaniment and requests were played for almost every ethnic group in the United States except the Irish.

Hughie made his first recording on disc in May 1937. Earlier, he had accompanied Coleman to one of his recording sessions and had been introduced to the studio proprietor. 'I'd like you to hear him', Coleman said. Hughie played and a formal recording session was arranged within a week. Four sides were recorded: *Master Crowley's Reels, The Irish Mazurka, The Mullingar Lee, The Star of Munster* and *McCormick's Hornpipe.* And so Hughie was launched to become one of the greatest traditional fiddle-players of all time.

And what of his style? Those of us who are prepared to listen feel in it the full expression of our pride and yearning, an exultant leap of the soul to God that is enshrined in that untranslatable Gaelic word, *duchas.*

In August 1986 there was a unique meeting in Hughie Gillespie's house, high up on that hill in the townland of Carrickmagrath. Assembled under his roof were three of his star pupils: Francie Kelly and two of my own sons, Paddy Og and Cathal. Hughie was not in the best of form and didn't feel like playing. However, he was very eager to listen. Francie hadn't his own fiddle with him but it wasn't long until the old king landed his own treasured instrument, the de Nicholas, in his lap. The three star pupils tuned up and started. It was a three-hour recital and never once did they repeat themselves.

Hughie sat there listening, a broad smile suffusing his countenance. Occasionally he took off the glasses and wiped away a tear. Somehow I sensed the same company would never meet again. His three princes were playing a farewell tribute to their monarch, although they may not have known it. They didn't spare themselves. It was, in truth, a bardic evening.

When eventually they stopped playing, Hughie rose, went over to Cathal, placed his right hand on his shoulder and said softly, but with great sincerity, 'Cathal, you're a great player!'

My mind went back to a night at the crossroads, Killygordon, during a *Comhaltas* session some twelve years before. The official session was long since over and Hughie was playing away with wonderful spirit and expertise. Music lovers hung around and seemed loath to leave. The inimitable Sean O'Gallchobhair, from Colm's sainted city, approached me. '*An geluineann tú Gillespie, a Pháidí?*' he exclaimed enthusiastically. '*Mar a duáirt Naomh Peadar ibhfad ó shin ag Athrú Crutha Íosa, A Mháistir, is maith duinn a bheith annseo.*' 'Paddy, do you hear Gillespie? As Saint Peter said yon time at the transfiguration of Jesus, "Master, it is good for us to be here!"'

Cathal went back to Canada. On Hallowe'en night, when the season of fruitfulness was dying, the good Lord found the single talent well employed and took Hughie to himself. There followed days of uncontrollable grief. As I stood by his grave in Sessiaghoneill graveyard and searched for words to express the feelings of those of us who knew and loved him, I was suddenly struck by the inadequacy of the English language.

Then the thought came to me that he was *not* dead. Hughie, old stock, you will never die. Wherever traditional fiddleplayers assemble to swap tunes and make music, you will be in their midst.

14

The Signal – Easter Snow

'That can't be him!' my brother Joe whispered. 'His trouser legs are too narrow. That man looks more like an overgrown Teddy-boy.'

'It is he, alright', I assured him, for the big man had started to whistle *Easter Snow*, which was to be the identifying signal.

We were standing outside the Laurel Tree in Kilburn. I approached the big man and saluted him. '*Go mbeannuigh Dia duit, A Sheamuis!*' I greeted him.

'*Dia agus Muire duit!*' he responded, and he thrust out a hand of welcome.

And so I met Seamus Ennis, singer, scholar, story-teller and piper par excellence. Truly, of him it could be said, 'And still they gazed and still the wonder grew that one small head could hold the tunes he knew.' But his genius was by no means confined to the head. It was manifested in the intricate and dexterous fingering of chanter, drones and regulator and in his rich and tasteful gracing of a tune.

Was there ever a musician could put such soul and beauty into the playing of that magnificent slow air, *Cois Abhann na Sead*, or bring such lift and vitality to the playing of *The Dingle Regatta* or *Flax in Bloom*?

That night we were welcomed by the proprietor of the Crown bar, a Geordie from Tyne-Tees country, and there we played music and sang until closing time. Seamus struck up a friendly relationship with Joe, who played an accordion, and it was surprising the number of tunes they played together.

I met him again in Ireland together with Joe Heaney, Willie Clancy and Brian Galligan, God rest them all. We sat on high stools and swapped songs in both languages until the grey daylight sent us scurrying to bed. It was one bardic night, I can tell you.

However, my abiding memory of our greatest traditional troubadour is on stage in the Royal Festival Hall, London, performing at an international folk-music concert. He came on stage and sat on a chair. He began leisurely strapping on and tuning the pipes, all the time regaling the audience with the legend of a famous piper the fairies had attempted to take away. They had lured him to a mountain-side and might have succeeded in stealing him entirely but for the fact that he had the presence of mind to stop walking, stand still, sign himself with the cross, take off his jacket and put it on again inside out.

'This ritual broke the stray spell they had put on him, and thanking God, he sat down on a rock and played this tune.'

The pipes were just in full tune as he finished the story. His timing was uncanny.

The last time I saw him was in Ollie Conway's pub in Mullagh. He was sitting in the centre of the room, surrounded by admirers, singing song after song of the big Munster love songs in his own mellifluous English translations. He stopped, rose to his full height and came towards me. He gave me a hearty handshake.

'Paddy Tunney, *The Stone Fiddle*, it is a book I'd love to have written!' he declared.

If the fairies failed to take him, the great God did not. Then why bewail his passing?

THE ROCK OF DOON
At dusk I saw a piper by the Rock of Doon
Beneath red rowans and the sickle of a moon
His fingers they were flying as he twiddle-twawed a
    tune
His wide eyes the wildest ever seen.
But ten times rarer than the rainbowed crock of gold
The haunting of the reel his chanter rolled

Of love and life eternal in a timeless land it told
To wee folk dancing on the green.

In double trebles wrought their feet in perfect mime
They rocked in riot as the music soared sublime
Above the swaying branches out beyond the reach of
    time
As piping spells that wizard spun anew.
Like beaten bronze their manes of flowing hair
Flung out like flame behind them on the moth-filled
    mountain air
I stood bewitched, bewildered and enchanted, I declare
As the wee feet trampled down the dew.

And when my spirit's restless and I wander wide
Where sea-nymphs beckon and the merfolk all abide
I leave the leering tyrant time alone to turn the time
And whisper to Charon on the shore.
Where, wading in the wantonness of sin and sudden
    death
He saps away the sinewed strength of mortals in
    a breath
Then I ride into eternity on white steed without greth
And grumble to God on high once more.

The hosts of heaven in a body all arise
With loud hosannas now they rake the domeless
    skies above
As sages such as Socrates and Plato in surprise
Forsake their wizened wisdom for a tune.
I lean and list for chanter and for drone
Our piper up in paradise no longer is unknown
Good people in the vale of tears no need to grieve
    or moan
For the piper who played at the Rock of Doon.

15

The Rodent Rebellion

Things were not looking good. Nazar had blocked the Suez Canal and there was a serious scarcity of petrol. We in the public health service of Donegal County Council were requested to travel as little as possible so as to conserve the few gallons of gasoline available. Rationing was introduced and ration books distributed. However, I was never asked for coupons at any of the filling stations when I called.

Doctor Maurice McParland was county medical officer in Donegal; a most astute and erudite officer he was, too, if I may say so, but he took panicky women much too seriously. Hence it happened when a female council tenant rang up and complained that there was a mass infestation of *ratus ratus* in her cockloft, he sent me a telegramme to proceed to Carn at once and to determine the degree of the infestation. It was 3.30 p.m. when the telegramme arrived. I rang the good doctor.

He instructed me to make the journey to Carndonagh, which is forty-two miles away, and to bring along a pocket torch as the shades of dusk would be falling no matter how fast I drove.

I set out in haste like the errant knights of old, but alas the beleaguered lady I was sent to succour was no Helen of Troy. I duly arrived at my destination, listened to the tale of woe from the lady in distress, got up a set of steps and boldly entered the alleged rodent stronghold through the ceiling trap-door. I discovered both to my relief and chagrin that the scampering up and down the ceiling had been done by a solitary mouse, and it was a field mouse too.

I am ashamed to say I dazzled the 'wee, sleekit, timorous

beastie' with the light and he submitted without a struggle.
One never places a mouse prisoner in irons, so I caught it
by the tail and threw it down the trap-door. Two cats were
waiting below to devour the poor thing.

I managed to convince the good lady that there were no
rats, or trace of rats, in her cockloft and she thanked God
fervently, but forgot about me.

When I was leaving she promised to pray for me. 'That
I won't run out of petrol on the way home?' I put the
question.

'That you won't run out of petrol will be my earnest
petition', she assured me. I felt greatly relieved, for the
same lady looked like one who would sing the psalms of
David backways on you.

On the way back I felt cold, hungry and desolate. Then
I remembered the doctor had requested a report on his
desk the following morning, even if it meant driving the
seventeen miles to the Lifford office with it and the rather
reckless consumption of petrol. 'By *Crom Cruaidh* and his
sub-gods twelve!' I swore, 'He'll get his report.' And he did.
Here it is.

THE ROYAL RATS OF CARN
Come all you gallant rodents that wander far and free
That shake a scut or crack a nut or bark a tall oak tree
Your brothers near Trabrega Bay are threatened in their
    warren
Leave friends and spouse and rush to rouse the Royal
    Rats of Carn.

It happened on a Sunday night not many moons ago
When dervishes from Donagh fair went dancing near
    to Doe
On their return their hearts did burn and quake with
    great alarm
For Royal Greys from Grianan Fort did hold their house
    in Carn.

The council sent a hero down, no piper pied was he
But practised on the pipes of Pan, and filled the rats
   with glee
They would not rout nor yet get out but deeper in
   they bored
Cuchuliann bade them '*oiche mhaith*' and vanished in
   his Ford.

With deep dismay these rats did say, 'No bloody spear
   he'll show
But grinning ghoul of weapon foul that coote used on
   Owen Roe
And phosphide fume will spell our doom where council
   men are tarrin'
In *sheugh* and ditch and boiling pitch will die the rats
   of Carn.'

They mailed an invitation out to Monty of Moville
Who bravely sent his Desert Rats to death on Long
   Stop Hill
Who burrowed in Bengazi sand near Bardia, bleak and
   barren
To come and lead a nobler breed, the Royal Rats of Carn.

He sent them back a curt reply and said he couldn't join
He might disturb a Billy boy who battled at the Boyne
Such tales of Irish rebel rats were sure to cause alarm
B-men and guards would fill jail yards with the Royal
   Rats of Carn.

They boldly did reply to him to be of great good cheer
The council had no Desert Fox to nip him in the rear
In days of yore a Billy king was master of their warren
They'd resurrect the conqueror to lead the rats of Carn.

The rodents mustered up their might, old grey-beards
   stern and tough
They came from every slaughterhouse from Malin town
   to Muff

They surged up from the bakehouses, the trade of war
  to learn
Upon that day the troops in grey did scare the folk in
  Carn.

The rabbits sent a wise old buck to pledge and promise
  aid
Their movement being underground, no troops would
  they parade
But brearded wheat in droves they'd eat in raids both
  bold and darin'
And field mice too would help to chew the hard grain
  stored in Carn.

A squirrel with a bushy tail from the woods above
  Drumboe
Declared they'd battle overhead while rabbits bored
  below
They would attack the healthy lines of spruce and
  Sitka tall
And take the life of every tree in royal Donegal.

The rats revealed their master plan to fortify the gates
They would invade the Lagan land and raise the council
  rates
If Major Chance would but advance they'd occupy his
  barn
Potato markets they'd control, the Royal Rats of Carn.

The clarion call rang loud and high from Derry to
  Culmore
And Norway rats from Baltic ships like Vikings swam
  ashore
Emblazoned on their shining shields were names like
  Grant and Farren
So forward to the barricades, Oh Royal Rats of
  Carn.

Doctor McParland displayed the report on the walls of his office and it was not removed until the public health offices were destroyed by fire some years later.

16

Billy Pigg: Piping Wizard of Northumbria

The sixties was a decade of great hope and promise for traditional singers and musicians in England and Scotland. Peter Kennedy's long-running series of the fifties under the title of *As I Roved Out*, compiled from field recordings made by Sean O'Boyle, Seamus Ennis, Spike Hughes and Kennedy himself, had enjoyed widespread popularity and was succeeded in the sixties by Ewan McColl's splendid *Radio Ballads* programme that reached across oceans and combed continents for rich and racy material. This was produced by Charles Parker, perhaps the finest producer of traditional programmes ever.

Bert Lloyd, now gone to God, had returned from his sheep-shearing and sugar-cane cutting exertions in far away Australia, whither he had gone to learn and record the folk-songs associated with these occupations, and was working like a beaver on top-quality folk programmes for the BBC.

At home, Ciaran MacMathuna and Sean MacReamonn were opening up the hidden Ireland to ever-increasing numbers of fascinated listeners. It was good to be alive, but to be young was very heaven!

Traditional singers were to the fore everywhere. Joe Heaney and Margaret Barry had taken London by storm, while others like the Wattersons, Anne Briggs, Bob Davenport, Frankie Armstrong, Luke Killen, Johnie Handel, Gordeanna McCullagh and our own Luke Kelly could be heard in England at least once a month.

Up in Dunedin, sometimes called Edinburgh, Hamish Mor Henderson had discovered Jeannie Robinson and was also presenting the Gaelic songs of the Western Isles to the people of Europe.

The Singers' Club in London, where Ewan MacColl and Peggy Seeger set the trend, was booked out, and all over the country from John O' Groats to land's end, folk-singing clubs were springing up.

It was Johnie Handel from Castle Garth, Newcastle-Upon Tyne, who first brought me to Geordie land. Johnie was a school-teacher, an accordionist, a guitarist, a piper, a singer, a raconteur, but above all, a gentleman.

I stayed with him and his charming wife at the Black Gate, Castle Garth, where his wife was curator of the museum, and every time the Royal Scotsman passed over the high level bridge, immortalised by Hill's hornpipe of the same name, the building heaved with the force of the vibration.

I had sung in the Royal Festival Hall, London, in 1958 and again in 1965, but did not penetrate Newcastle until 1967. On that occasion the weight of song I was forced to unload upon them was nothing short of staggering. So much so, in fact, that there was little time for visiting or sightseeing.

In the spring of 1968 I was back again, but my load was considerably lightened by my brother Joe! He was a smashing box-player, a good singer and a renowned traditional step-dancer. No wonder I felt free to relax and enjoy my spell among the Geordies.

We performed every other night, and on our free days we were brought away to Hadrian's Wall, the Cheviot Hills or the Middle Marches. We visited de Solis's castle, a grim and forbidding ruin just across the border in bonnie Scotland where Mary, Queen of the Scots, was reputed to have visited one of her admirers who had been severely wounded in a duel with another warrior. She rode eighty miles in one day to see him, and it is said that he was restored to health shortly afterwards.

De Solis was a Norman knight, well versed in the mysteries and magic of the black art. So wicked was this man and so heinous were his crimes that the foundation of his castle was supposed to have sunk nearly two feet. The charge was also made against him that he sacrificed infants and small children to mollify the prince of darkness. He had to be destroyed. This could only be done by enclosing him in a leaden coffin, submerging the coffin in a cauldron of boiling oil, and finally throwing the coffin into a river of rushing water.

And so they put a sleeping potion in his wine and while he slept they sealed him in a coffin of lead, boiled it in the bubbling oil and then dumped the coffin into the nearest spate river. That river hissed and spluttered, and the heat of the leaden coffin and the knightly demon within dried up half the water. Then the coffin lid flew off, releasing seven horned, tailed and cloven-footed devils that vanished in a sheet of flame and were never seen in the Middle Marches again.

De Solis they found to be very dead indeed, but when they brought him for a Christian burial, the sanctified soil thrice threw him up. At length he was interred in unconsecrated ground, and seven heavy granite slabs laid over his grave. Only an earthquake could dislodge such a weight of stone, and to date no earth tremors have disturbed his unquiet rest in the Middle Marches.

At a later date when archaeologists excavated the site, it was found that a faulty foundation was the cause of the subsidence. Nevertheless, an inordinate number of infant skeletons were uncovered. They had not been offered in sacrifice. Historical researchers familiar with the region and the exigencies of the time are convinced that the castle was the abortion centre for the entire Tyne-Tees–Middle Marches territory.

We left the precincts of the castle and drove over the access road leading to it. As we reached the point where the old drawbridge once gave access to the castle, the front left wheel fell off Luis Killen's Volkswagon. The jinx associated with the place had been visited upon us! We jacked up the car, replaced the wheel and continued our descent.

At a little hamlet half-way down the hills, we stopped for refreshments. I had been trying to pick up a famous border ballad telling the sad story of a young Jacobite laird, lured away to London, thrown in the Tower and finally hanged for his support of Prince Charlie at the battle of Culloden. As we began a game of dominos I asked Louis Killen to sing it again and he duly obliged. There were two hard-bitten shepherds sipping brown ale over by the fire. One of them straightened up on his chair and listened attentively until the ballad was sung. He then rose and with tears in his eyes approached us.

'It was terrible, terrible about the young laird', he began.

'God's curse on the Sasanach!'

'Amen!' I prayed and shook his calloused hand. He left, a smile of satisfaction suffusing his rugged face.

'There's hope for merry England yet', I told the two Tynesiders.

'Tunney, you'll have us all hanged yet with your treason and your teasin', Handel warned me.

'What about your North-East Republic?'

'Just a pipe dream.'

'And the Jarrow march?'

'Just a march. How could it be anything else, you bugga', and he proceeded to light his pipe.

'Dream away', I ribbed him, 'But when are we going to visit Billy Pigg?'

'This very night', he replied and puffed away at the pipe.

'You should have told me', I pleaded.

'I was keeping it for an after-dinner surprise.'

So after dinner we set out for Wood Hill Farm just outside Hepple in the foothills of the Cheviots, the home of the one and only Billy Pigg, prince of Northumbrian pipers. There were seven of us trussed into Louis Killen's Beetle Volkswagon: Louis Killen himself, Johnie Handel, Jim Glenndenning, my brother Joe, myself and two *céilí*-dancing Newcastle girls.

A bardic night it turned out to be with piping, melodeon-playing and singing and dancing on a plane we never succeeded in reaching since. Maybe Billy had inscribed an invisible druidic circle on the floor prior to our arrival. Of this I am certain. Every one of us was bewitched that night.

It was night-falling when we reached our destination. Billy was waiting for us at the gable-end of the house and ushered us into a room that was broader than it was long. Johnie Handel did the introductions and in no time at all we relaxed and were chatting away merrily. At the mention of Ireland, Billy exclaimed, 'Ah yes! Willie Clancy, Frank McPeake, Leo Rowsome and Seamus Ennis. Great pipers!'

There were bottles of hard stuff, six-packs of brown ale appearing out of great coat pockets and ladies hold-alls, and we were introduced to Billy's own home-brewed cider. My brother Joe and I regaled ourselves with draughts of the most delicious spring-well water I ever tasted, if one is to exclude the water from Tom Harte's well in Keadue in the county of Rosscommon.

The door opened and in marched a big gangley rung of a man with a shepherd's crook and a fiddle case. His name was Jack Elliot and he played the fiddle.

'Honestly, Billy', he began, 'I can only stay a while. I'm lambing this weather and if I'm not around a man could lose a lamb or two.' We nodded sympathy with a man in such a predicament.

'Bring out the fiddle, anyhow', Billy coaxed him, 'I don't like starting on my own.' He did so and Billy tuned up the pipes.

He sat on a chair in the middle of the floor, fixed his audience with a puckish grin and began to play. It was obvious from the very start that Elliot was playing second fiddle. Pigg was the performer par excellence. His first touch of the chanter transformed the room into a Merlin's Cave, and the spell of music he wove held us enthralled.

The shepherd looked at his watch and dashed off to his ewes in labour, but Billy played on. It was a dazzling performance. He ranged through a medley of hornpipes, jigs and reels that included *Hill's High Level*, *The Exhibition*

Hornpipe, and Billy Pigg's *The Random Jig, Father O'Flynn* and *The Last of the Twins*.

When he switched to a wild and wonderful setting of *The Swallow's Tail* my feet got the better of me. A leap and a bound and there I was on the hearth-rug paving away with complete abandon until I collapsed with exhaustion into a chair.

The Geordies were petrified. What had I done? Billy left down his pipes and applauded. Handel and Killen breathed great sighs of relief.

'You're a wizard!' I exclaimed. 'That was pure magic! I had to dance.'

'I know, I know,' he assured me, 'and you danced well.'

It was only when we were going back to Newcastle that night my friends informed me I had committed a sacrilege. 'You rent the Veil of the Temple and trampled on the Ark of the Covenant. You danced on Billy Pigg's Golden Fleece. And he applauded! You Irish get away with murder. I have seen him clear the room just because some blundering Geordie accidentally stepped on that sheepskin!' Handel told me solemnly.

When supper-time came Billy treated us to tea, home-made bread, butter and cheese he himself pressed together, and a great variety of jams and jellies made by Mrs Pigg herself. I was tempted to think of Devine away up in the Sperrins above the market of sweet Strabane:

I will press my cheese while my wool's a' teasing
My ewes I'll milk by the break o' day
While the whirring moorcock and lark allures me
Oh! Moorlough Mary, won't you come away.

We went back to the music, the songs and dances and it was 4.00 a.m. before we left Wood Hall. Billy Pigg played set-dances, polkas and Irish tunes, such as *The Gentle Maiden* and *The Lark in the Clear Air*.

However, it is in the Scottish tunes and laments and in the slow music of the border region that the unique genius of

Pigg is truly manifested. There is a wild, lonesome other-worldliness about his playing of these pieces that transports the listener to a world beyond the corridors of time. It may well be that the music of the garden of Eden fell out of time's pocket before Adam's downfall and circled around the universe until captured and recycled by the wizardry of Billy Pigg. It is a music that haunts and fills one with an insatiable yearning for a lost long ago:

For Oh! I heard the music, and answered to the call
Now the sea wind mocks my longing, but the land wind
    saddens all.

It was with bitter grief and a deep sense of loss that I heard of Billy Pigg's death in October of the same year. There must have been a scarcity of pipers in paradise, for he just predeceased many of our own great pipers. Surely they must meet – Clancy, Rowsome, McPeake and Ennis – to swap tunes and yarns with the inimitable Pigg in 'that world beyond the world's end, where nothing is but glee.'

17

The Golden Lands

Gold is where you find it, they say, and for those searching for the rare metal through songs in the idiom of the people there remains many precious nuggets still to be unearthed in my native County Fermanagh.

From Lisnaskea to Donagh Cross, through Ballagh and Dernawilt to Rosslea and round by Easnadarragh, you will find home-spun songs to match and master those of any other part of this little island.

Take, for instance, *Edward Boyle*, a song from the Rosslea area. Is there a better example of a lover pining for her sweetheart, gone into exile in the land of the free across the Western ocean?

EDWARD BOYLE
You tender-hearted Christians of high and low degree
Likewise you wounded lovers, come sympathise with
    me
For it's here I'm left bewailing a young man I adore
He's now fled from my arms, bound for Columbia's
    shore.

Right well do I remember it being in the month of May
When nature's flowery mantle does bedeck the meadows
    gay
When everything seems charming, bright fortune it did
    smile
When I parted with my own true love, my charming
    Edward Boyle.

In the county of Fermanagh and the parish of Rosslea

In the townland of Grawarren near the mountain of
   Lough Beagh
He was reared by honest parents who each day for him
   did toil
But now they're sunk in sorrow for the loss of Edward
   Boyle.

'Twas on a Monday morning his friends did him convey
All to the town of Dundalk and from there down to the
   quay
With courage bold he did set sail and left the Shamrock
   shore
May joys attend you, Edward; will I ever see you more?

His friends they are all lonesome since young Edward
   went away
He was the pride of college, and the flute so well could
   play
His neighbours all both great and small, they swear to
   leave this isle
In hopes once more on Columbia's shore to seek out
   Edward Boyle.

My curse attend Columbus who first went to that shore
Likewise that ship Emerigo that sailed in days of yore
From that time down so many are bound in sorrow,
   grief and toil
To lament and mourn their love's return like me and
   Edward Boyle.

So to conclude and finish, all you fair maids who are
   true
Don't ever place your minds on gold as lovers sometimes
   do
For if I possessed the wealth and store that's in Saint
   Patrick's Isle
I would part it all and ten times more for one glimpse of
   Edward Boyle.

Then, of course, when we enter the woods of that lovely county and wander by the shores of the lough most mentioned in the annals and poetry of our country, the lapping of water on limestone flags induces a oneness with nature that invariably breaks out in song. Here, in bygone years, men hunted and fished and occasionally poached game in the preserves of the landlords and estate owners.

When caught and transported to Van Deimen's land, their lovers pined and sorrowed for them at home. Here is a very good sample of the kind of song in which they gave vent to their grief and longing. Curious that another Edward is the hero in this instance, but you will find that the two male names predominating in most Fermanagh traditional songs are Edward and Willie, or William.

This song is a favourite of Rita Gallagher, the linnet from the Blue Stacks. Pauline Sweeney of Crossroads, Killygordon, thrice All-Ireland singing queen, who ceased competing in order to give others a chance, also had high regard for it.

EDWARD, ON LOUGH ERNE SHORE

The sun was setting behind yon mountain, the dew was
    falling upon the lea
And I was seated beside a fountain; a feathered warbler
    sang on a tree
With loves and kisses his notes were sounding, made me
    reminded of days of yore
When in a bower I plucked a flower and dreamed of
    Edward on Lough Erne shore.

A crop of sorrow I will reap tomorrow, my rose is fading
    and my hopes decay
For it's in the night time when all are sleeping, awake
    I'm weeping till the break of day
Delight has fled me and woe has wed me, why did you
    leave me, my love *a stóir*?

For love is golden, and bonniest Edward would not
  forsake me on Lough Erne shore.

Oh, the cuckoo's notes in the air are sounding, a song so
  fleeting to please the ear
And every note is a bliss abounding, here in this valley
  if he was near
Each step I take by the winding river where we have
  wandered in days of yore
Reminds me of Edward, my banished lover, who left me
  lonely on Lough Erne shore.

Oh, could I move like a moon o'er the ocean I would
  send a sigh o'er the distant deep
Or could I fly like a bird in motion; by my Edward's
  side I would ever keep
I would fondly soothe him, with songs amuse him; our
  feelings fuse them; he'd sigh no more
And seven long years they would soon pass over; then
  we'd both live happy on Lough Erne shore.

18

Of Bog and Road and the Crying Wind

I recall Father Lorcan O'Ciaran, once parish priest of Templecarn, saying that Padraic Colum must have had the *sheughs* and bogs of Derryhallow in mind when he wrote his famous *Old Woman of the Roads* and *The Drover*.

The last of the great patriarch priests and one of the fathers of Sinn Fein may not have been far out, for Master Kane once told me that Colum's wife was a McGuire from Derryhallow. Her father lived in the snug farmstead subsequently acquired by Frank Monaghan whose family still resides there. He went on to inform me that the good woman's father was none other than Sergeant James McGuire of the RIC, who arrested Father McFadden, the patriot priest, in Gweedore one Sunday morning when Sub-Inspector Martin was slain with a paling stab for attempting the same act. The master went on to describe how the hand that arrested Father McFadden withered like a blighted potato stalk and was of no further use to the rash sergeant.

There is no written record of the withered hand in the histories of that period, but then the memories and hearts of the people often preserve the truth more accurately than the arid records of fusty old historians.

The fact that Colum's wife hailed from Derryhallow would give credence to Father Lorcan's supposition. During the seventies, Derryhallow School, once my *alma mater*, was the venue of many rousing *Comhaltas Ceoltóirí Éireann* concerts, and the singing, dancing and music went on into the small hours.

Brendan Faughnan, respectfully referred to as the master, my brother Joe, Mick Hernon, Mary Ellen and Hughie

O'Connor were the prime movers behind these displays of our native culture.

Among the many outside artists performing, there was the great Hughie Gillespie, Francie Kelly, Sean Lee and the famous fluting singer, Cathal McConnell. A versatile artist, McConnell was also an expert on the tin whistle. However, it is as one of my favourite traditional singers I always remember him. His singing of *The Flower of Sweet Erin the Green*, the poignant narrative of a lovelorn maiden who misplays a well-dealt hand, never fails to stir the hearts of those who still swear allegiance to Cupid. Here it is:

THE FLOWER OF SWEET ERIN THE GREEN
Draw near each young lover, lend ear to my ditty
That hears my sad mournful tale
Come join me in consort and lend me your pity
While I my misfortune bewail.
The grief of my poor heart no tongue can disclose
My cheeks are now pale that once blushed like the rose
And it's all for a young man whom I do suppose
Is now far from sweet Erin the green.

Ah sure, when we were children we walked out
     together
Along the green valleys so neat
Although we were childish we loved one another
Whilst plucking the wild berries sweet.
It was in sweet Arvey we both went to school
He was first in his class and correct in each rule
And I cheerfully walked home through old Kilmacool
With the flower of sweet Erin the green.

His head on my bosom he often reposed it
Each evening all under a shade
And a song in my praises, my darling composed it
And styled me the Colederry maid.
The night that I denied him, I'd die for his sake
It was little I thought my denial he'd take

Ah, but to my misfortune I made a mistake
When he left me in Erin the green.

Ah, it's little I thought that my darling would leave me
No matter what I'd say or do
For he oft times told me he ne'er would deceive me
But vowed to be constant and true.
But I need not blame him for breaking these laws
For to my misfortune I myself was the cause
And his truth and his honesty will gain him applause
When he's far from sweet Erin the green.

So come all you young maids of this dear Irish nation
I pray you be steady and wise
And likewise give ear to my kind assertation
And never your true love despise.
For such foolish folly distracted I rave
There is no peace for me but yon dark, silent grave
And all hope denied me, I'll soon take my lave
Of the flower of sweet Erin the green.

And then my brother Joe would be called upon to sing.
Invariably, he gave us *The Mountains of Pomeroy* as only Joe
could sing it. Old fires were fanned into flame where the
last gleed of hope had been *greeshaghed* in dispair. Blood
quickened and heads were held erect again. Who would dare
to say that our *mórtas cine* had been finally extinguished?

That song with its proud defiance always puts me in mind
of Douglas McGinley, the kilted barrister who had spent
his life in love with and in labour for his language and
his country, as he stood on the stage of the Abbey Hall in
Ballyshannon, proclaiming *The Outlawed Raparee*:

My spurs are rusty, my coat is torn, my plume is dank
  with rain
And the thistle down and the barley beard are thick on
  me
But my rifle's as bright as my true love's eye and my
  arm is strong and free

Oh what care I for their king and laws, I'm an outlawed
  Raparee!

THE MOUNTAINS OF POMEROY

The dawn was springing fresh and fair, the lark sang in
  the sky
When the maid, she bound her golden hair with a
  bright glance in her eye
For who beyond yon high green wood was awaiting
  her with joy
Oh, whom but her gallant Reynardine, on the mountains
  of Pomeroy.

Chorus:
An outlawed man in a land forlorn, he scorns to turn
  and fly
But keeps the flag of freedom safe among the mountains
  high.

How often in the dawning hour, how oft in the twilight
  brown
He met the maid in the green wood shade where the
  streams came tumbling down
For they were constant in a love no foe could e'er
  destroy
No tyrant breed touched Reynardine, in the mountains
  of Pomeroy.

'My love,' she said, 'I am sore afraid of the foemens'
  wrath for you
They have traced you by the lonely heights and all the
  valleys through
My kinsmen frown when you are named; your life they
  would destroy
"Beware", they say, "of Reynardine on the mountains of
  Pomeroy."'

He said, 'My dear, you must never fear of your
  kinsmens' hate for me

No tyrant's thrall can e'er befall the arm that will be free
But leave your cruel kin and come where the lark is in
the sky
And with my gun I'll guard you on the mountains of
Pomeroy.'

The maid arose and fast she fled from her cruel kin and
home
And bright the flood and rosy red the tumbling torrents
foam
But a mist came down and a storm came on and did all
around destroy
And a pale, drowned bride met Reynardine on the mountains
of Pomeroy.

My sister Annie Lunny, who subsequently lost her life
in a tragic fire at her home, would then be prevailed upon
to sing one of Fermanagh's loveliest songs, *The Buachaill
Roe.*

THE BUACHAILL ROE
Come all you loyal heroes and listen unto me
And I'll sing you a verse or two of my love's destiny
For the lad I loved so dearly from my arms is forced to
go
Still I own I love him dearly, he's my charming
Buachaill Roe.

Chorus:
Oh, the gentle thrush forsakes the bush
And the blackbird hovers low
With a cry of desolation that bewails my Buachaill Roe
Oh, the gentle thrush forsakes the bush
And the blackbird hovers low
Still, I own I loved him dearly, he's my charming
Buachaill Roe.

He was a youth undaunted, his age was twenty-three

And for to search this nation round, his equal ne'er
   you'd see
With two black eyes and rosy cheeks, his skin as white
   as snow
But I own I loved him dearly, he's my charming
   Buachaill Roe.

He was a youth undaunted, of courage and noble blood
And for the cause of Ireland on the battlefield he stood
He never once retreated, though his wounds were deep
   and sore
Still, I own I loved him dearly, he's my charming
   Buachaill Roe.

The Erne is now closed by a heavy mist of rain
And so is Enniskillen, where my true love does remain
I'll build my true love's castle on the banks of Lough
   Erne shore
And I'll plant the woods with laurels for my charming
   Buachaill Roe.

Then a forestry inspector's wife would oblige with a song
she called *Come Over the Hill*, which she sang to the tune of
Buachaill O'n Eirne, and Eddie Lawn would delight us with
the fate that befell him when he bought trousers in Belcoo.
It appears he bought them on the *ceannt* there and they were
surplus stock from the wardrobe of a Billy boy. How else
would Eddie cheer for King William and the red, white and
blue if they hadn't been an Orangeman's trousers?

In 1979 when it was Joe's turn to leave us lonely and
grief-stricken in this valley of tears, the poignant words of
my mother's song came back to me. They were, of course,
found in *Mo Drathereen Ó Mo Chroí*. Here is the song:

MO DRATHEREEN Ó MO CHROÍ, OR LITTLE BROTHER OF
MY HEART
The womb's turned to earth that gave birth to my
   brother and me

And likewise my father has gone to eternity
Like babes in the forest, now poor orphan children
  are we
Which makes me lament for my *dratbereen ó mo chroí.*

When we were young, we did each other adore
This little green island we rambled it o'er and o'er
We wrought at our trades and our money we spent it
  quite free
Which makes me lament for my *dratbereen ó mo chroí.*

He went to the war where proud England united with
  France
His regiment was first in the red battle ranks to advance
Where cannons do roar and shot and shell do fly
Perhaps in that battle my *dratbereen* oh does lie.

Now I'm alone like the desolate bird of the night
This world and its beauty no longer afford me delight
The dark, narrow grave is the only sad refuge for me
Since I lost my heart's darling, my *dratbereen ó mo chroí.*

19

Near the Mountain Streams

All week the wind blew down Lough Swilly, and from Farsetmore to Malin Head the rain sheets bellied out like the sails of some phantom ship fleeing away from the land of the O'Donnells. Who sailed those ghost ships: the *Sluagh Shee* commanded by Mannan Mac Lir, or the spirits of long dead Vikings doomed to re-enact one of their savage raids on the fair land of Tirconnell?

Fair it was and fair it remained even in that bleak and blustery August of 1980. From Drumerdagh near Letterkenny all the way down the Lagan to Burnfoot, the fields rippled with ripening barley. Standing sentinel over those lush and fertile lands is the *Grianan of Aileach* where, in a secret hall beneath its ramparts, the warriors of old lean on their spears and sleep, waiting for the clarion call that will summon them to drive the gall forever from the sacred soil of Ireland.

It was Thursday and the *Scoil Eigse*, sponsored by *Comhaltas Ceoltoiri Éireann*, had brought students trooping from Britain, Europe and the land of the free beyond the Western ocean to flavour the songs, stories and music that are part and parcel of our priceless heritage here in this island:

> Songs of our land, you are with us forever
> The power and the splendour of thrones pass away
> But yours is the might of some fast-flowing river
> O'er summer's bright roses and autumn's decay.

How well does the blind poet Frances Browne, from Stranorlar on the banks of the Finn, convey to us the full

force and indestructibility of our traditional songs in one
powerful verse!

True, the friars across the sea from sunny France had not
come, but nevertheless the French, the Dutch, the Spanish
and the Germans were there in strength, learning to sing, play
music and dance in ways almost as old as original sin. Was it
presumption then that prompted me to ponder on the great
schools of Bangor, Clonard and Clonmacnoise?

I was on my way up from the Lake of Shadows Hotel,
where the clash of armour had wrested me rudely from
the arms of Morpheus the night before. Suits of armour
and swords and shields should not decorate the walls and
landings of inns when high-spirited young Claremen and
Dubliners are about.

Jimmie McBride shouted to me from the steps of Dun
Emer, his stately abode.

'The weather's wild. We must appease the gods of Kinnago. Their wrath will wreck the *fleadh*!'

'When will we make the *turus*?' I inquired.

'This very night', he told me. 'Sure, Pat's preparing for
us all week! Mum's the word, of course. We don't want a
whole trevalley landing in on him. You and Conal O'Donnell
can come with me. Jimmie McFarland will fetch the two
McDaids. Do you think Sarah Ann O'Neill, Mary Bergin and
Joe Burke would squeeze into Seamus McMathuna's bus?
It's no Rolls Royce, I know, but it will hold the four of them.'

'Of course it will. I have seen more people than that
emerging from it.'

'That number would be just about right. I'll collect the
six-packs early in the Brass Rail.'

As dusk descended we slipped out of Buncrana and
headed for the slow, torturous climb into the hills of dark
Innishowen. The road was long, but as Tom Keown said to
Mrs Deary long ago at the house-dance in Tonnaghgorn, it
was narrow.

Conal O'Donnell consoled us with the remark that the
road to heaven was steep and narrow, and indeed that the

old people in the Gaeltacht always maintained there were a right lock of lubs in it too.

Pat Mulhern, the renowned minstrel of Innishowen, stood by the half-door to greet us as we tumbled out of the cars. At eighty-five he was still as straight as a yard of pumped water and his singing, in the old measured style of Ulster, could still hold an audience captive for hours. Like all good traditional performers, he prefaced most of his big songs with the story of its origin and a graphic account of the song-carrier who passed it on to him.

As a fiddle-player he was even then the last of the old music masters in the peninsula, and he numbered among his pupils the dancing fiddle-player Dinny McLaughlin, of royal descent, and the indefatigable John McCracken.

'Do you see the light over in Shandrum, Paddy?' he asked me. 'That's Dinny's. He used to travel the whole way over here when he was a caddie for music lessons. And McCracken, he aye came on a wheel. Troth indeed, they were two good pupils.'

We were not long in Pat Mulhern's kitchen when the fun began. It was a mighty siege of singing that would rout the most stubborn ghosts of gloom. Jimmie McFarland was the first call and he sang Cathal McConnel's version of *The Mountain Streams*. This invariably led to the singing of my mother's version and indeed that of the great Denis Cassley from Glenshesk, now gone to God. All three songs have different tunes, but the words are basically the same. It is an Ulster song unknown in the other provinces of Ireland until we sang it there.

Pat himself sang *The Clear, Winding Ayr* and then asked for my mother's version of the same song. I duly obliged. John McDaid, enthroned in the big chair in the corner, emptied his glass and, employing that puckish Billy Pigg grin that transfixes audiences, he wound *The Flower of Moville, Young Dinsmur of Bonnie Woodhall* and the delightful *Rose of the Finn*.

It was then Conal O'Donnell's turn to tell us of missed

opportunities in that lovely old song *Geaftai Bhaile Bui* and to set us laughing with a racy rendition of *An Sean Duine Dóite*.

Seamus McMathuna brought us on a global trip in his hilarious *Glen Lee* and Jimmie McBride reminded us of the grim days of eviction and its attendant miseries with songs relating to the liquidation of one Sub-Inspector Martin who was fool-hardy enough to attempt to arrest the land league hero, Father James McFadden.

Sarah Ann O'Neill followed with that hauntingly beautiful exile song, *Dobbin's Flowery Dale*, and Pat McDaid sang the defiant song *Pat O'Donnell. Craigie Hill, The Banks of Dunmore, Moorlough Mary, Lough Erne Shore* and *Easter Snow* also got favourable mention.

When a trill of triplets fountained from Mary Bergin's whistle, the *fear a' ti* remarked it was as well the birds of the air in the ash tree outside were asleep.

'If it were daytime and them blackbirds heard that music they'd go clane out of their minds with jealousy and tear every *cuinneog* of thatch off my roof for the down dint of spite!'

But it was when Joe Burke strapped on his accordion and cut loose in the irrepressible *Bucks of Oranmore* that things began to happen in earnest. The big door was open and the music drifted out over the quiet mountainside.

Seamus McMathuna, abroad in the gable field at the time, burst in and declared excitedly that he had seen the great god Pan himself dance on a flat flag in the light of the moon.

Pat Mulhern laughed. 'That'll be my ram you saw', he told Seamus. 'I got him when he was a young lamb from a sheep-man over near Drung. His mother had died and I reared him up on a bottle. He got a wee thing petted and used to be in here on the floor when I'd be playing the fiddle. He had aye a great conceit in reels and in no time at all started keeping time to them with his cleets. Man dear, the next thing I noticed he was up on the hind legs dancing away there like a Christian. Damn, but that ram's full of music. Curious thing though, jigs, hornpipes and Highlands

don't seem to excite him at all. But he's not nearly as good
a dancer as he used to be. Them sixty ewes have taken the
steam out of him, do you see!'

'But the creature I saw dancing out there looked like a
goat-man!' Seamus stuck to his guns.

'Did you chance to remark if it had horns?' Pat queried
him.

'Horns!' exclaimed Seamus, 'He had a pair of antlers!'

'Then it was my ram you saw. Sure, that Pan of yours is a
polly, isn't he!'

Still, Pat's ram was not the only animate thing to fall under
the spell of Burke's *Bucks of Oranmore*. Scarcely had he started
up again after the bit of commotion, than four of us leaped
out on the floor and began flaking out a traditional reel with
utter abandon. It was in the course of that dance that we
discovered the clinker in Pat's floor.

'Now the clinker was a special flag set centrewise in the
flagged floor of a kitchen. There was a hollow left under it
into which sometimes a horse's skull was affixed. By reason
of the flag's texture, the hollow it covered and the horse's
head therein, the flag emitted a pleasant ring, or clink, when
struck by the hobnails in the boots of expert dancers. It was
on this clinker that champion reel-dancers met to execute the
heel shuffle and half-turn at the end of each part of a reel tune,
prior to the heel pivot. It was used to illustrate the virtuosity
of the good reel-dancers who were said to be able to 'turn on
a sixpenny piece'.

Pat Mulhern's kitchen is perhaps the only one in Ireland
to preserve the clinker flag in all its pristine splendour. And
we had discovered it by accident!

  Bind sultry silence in thongs of thunder, and ropes of
      laughter round the rigging sweel
  Across the flagstone where dancers pivot, their hobnails
      rivet a rousing reel
  All fiddle-frensied the feet are flying, and legs are lacing
      in a thousand loops

Now fast they're wheeling to face the music, and
handclaps hail them and lusty whoops.

The man of the house had the last call. We stood on his
kitchen floor and proclaimed the anthem of the gentle and
genial Joe Holmes, *Good Friends and Companions*, and then
Pat sang for us in his inimitable style that fine song, *Dark
Innishowen*:

An old man bred in the mountain marrow, stood up to
harrow where the dancers ploughed
A troubadour from the heights of glory, he told his story
of love aloud.
The *greeshagh* glows, the strong month quivers, from
throat there rivers like rain in drought
A song that leaps down the lanes of longing, and hones
a hunger for the land of youth.

Whether it was Pat's pet ram or the great god Pan which
danced in the moonlight near the shadow of Kinnago will
never be firmly established. The wrath of the gods were most
certainly appeased, for the next day the sun broke through
and spilled light and delight on the crowds who gathered in
Buncrana for the music and song of the *fleadh*.

Let us leave Pat Mulhern, then, in a world that hasn't
changed much since the dawn of creation. He'll have the
thrush and blackbird to tell him of the spring's return. A
hawk hovering over the purple heather of the mountainside
will hang motionless in the air to drop like a shooting star
on its prey.

The hay haggard in harvest will fill with a chatter of
sparrows, and a crow, or perhaps a raven, will darken the
red berries of the rowan during the snows of winter. Come
spring, come summer, come autumn or winter, Pat will ever
hear the linnet sing her sweet notes so pleasing near the
mountain streams where the moorcocks crow.

20

Céilí in the Clouds

It was 1976. The previous year I had moved to Galway for reasons I am not completely certain about even to this day. Maybe it was just that my family were rapidly approaching university age and that a base in Galway would suit the family unit much better than one in Donegal. With the death of my mother that same year there seemed to be little left in Ulster. On the other hand, the great *seán-nós* singers of Connemara were still very much alive and singing.

The great republic over the Western ocean was celebrating two-hundred years of independence. Ethnic groups from many European countries were invited to Washington D.C. by the Smithsonian Institution, brought there to perform in the idiom of the people they represented. I happened to be one of a group of twenty-three persons selected to let out traditional light shine in the land discovered by Christopher Columbus.

We were advised to take neither staff, nor food, nor bed, nor money. Neither were we to have two coats, just a light shower-proof one to protect us from the summer squalls that not infrequently blew up from the Gulf of Mexico. Ciaran MacMathúna and the eminent folklorist Tom Munnelly were entrusted with the task of recruiting and marshalling the Irish traditional shock troops, and a fair job they made of it too.

So, early on a Sunday morning we assembled on the tarmac of Shannon Airport to be borne by a jumbo jet to the shores of Americay. The trip generated a degree of excitement among us, it cannot be denied.

After dinner I settled down to read *An Bealach* by the

Spanish priest who founded *Opus Dei*, but soon fell fast asleep. I was wakened by Ciaran MacMathúna who escorted me to the back of the plane where a Clare set was in full swing. It was followed by a high caul cap in which I danced, and the *céilí* in the clouds continued with reels, Highlands and polkas. We had just finished the *Stack of Barley* when, to my horror, I noticed our pilot in the circle of onlookers, obviously enjoying himself.

He read the concern on my face and came over. 'Don't worry, old chap', he assured me. 'Automatic control has taken over, at least for the moment.' I thanked him and began to demonstrate the intricacies of the mazurka to Maeve Donnelly, for I have absolute confidence in Aer Lingus pilots.

And then we sighted some ice floes off the Canadian coast. I was called upon to sing *The Green Fields of Canada*, but it was quite impossible to be heard over the giant throb of the jet engines.

We continued down the Eastern Coast of Canada, leaving a white vapour trail in our wake, and when we touched down at Kennedy Airport you could literally fry an egg on the pavement. But it was a sultry heat, one like that occasionally felt at home in Ireland before a thunder-storm. It was much hotter and oppressive, of course. We taxied away in a small plane to an airport near Washington D.C. and hence by bus to Georgetown University in the federal capital.

The storm struck. It was a wonderful sight. Lightning skivered down the sky and thunder peals shook the earth and air. It rained bullock stirks and beetles and the road metal was ripped up and swept away in the floods. Two of the Clare set-dancers reached for their rosaries and began to recite the prayers for the dying. It did look like the beginning of the end of the world. However, the deluge ceased as suddenly as it began and the sun winked an eye at us just before night fell.

At Harmon House, Georgetown, I shared a room with Big Sonnie McDonagh, the flute player from Bunanadden in the county of Sligo, and we didn't need to be rocked asleep.

We woke bright and early next morning. I opened the shutters and looked out. There was brilliant sunshine and a temperature of ninety-two degrees Fahrenheit. Two black men were tearing round the running track as if their lives depended on the length and speed of each stride.

'What do they mean?' Sonnie put the question to me, 'Bursting their backsides running out there! Wouldn't it fit them better to be away digging the spuds for the dinner?' I agreed but made bold to suggest that their spuds might not be fit for digging yet. 'Faith, and if they are not I hope they have them well sprayed. Another day with the lunk heat of last night and the blight will blacken every stalk they are growing. It never occured to either of us that the men might never have tasted the flavour of a Kerr's Pink or a Catherionie in their lives.

After a day's orientation, which consisted of warnings to steer clear of certain areas of the city lest perhaps we witness the abject poverty existing there, we began our forenoon and afternoon concerts on the Irish pavilion, erected along the banks of the Reflecting Pool between the Washington and Lincoln memorials. A number of other pavilions were erected for the other groups, but for some strange reason we Irish drew the biggest crowds. We performed there every day for ten days and in the evenings were the guests of the Irish ambassador and diverse Irish-American senators, their wives and their overgrown daughters, who were members of the Democratic Party, of course.

Then we went on tour, visiting Philadelphia; Chicago; Fort Dodge, Iowa; Baltimore; and New York. Nothing much happened in Philadelphia. We were, of course, presented with a replica of the Liberty Bell with its famous split, and there was a conducted tour of the Benjamin Franklin Museum, but hail and thunder hindered our open-air performance in the city of friends.

Things came very much alive in the windy city. I found it

to be a friendly, youthful, vibrant place. Mike Maloney will tell you they still speak in whispers about my blistering runs in baseball games in that city.

The second night there, a mighty banquet was held in our honour in the garden of one Niall Sheridan, a wealthy Irish-American and a much-decorated war veteran. Half-way through the banquet, a slight difference of opinion developed between our road manager, an overbearing German-American, and a strong-willed member of our party, which was finally resolved when they cop-carlied into the swimming-pool.

As they waltered and splashed about in the pool, pouring scorn and calumny on to each other's heads, I spied a wistful and wonderful-looking female creature standing on the edge of the crowd with a bewildered look on her well-chiselled features. A fair maiden in distress? I sprang to attention and hurried to her side.

She carried a fiddle-case and I took my cue from it.

'You play the fiddle, or should I say the violin?'

'The fiddle only', came the reply. She was winsome and willowy and completely unspoiled.

'And you sing, no doubt?'

'I do.'

'American folk-songs?'

'Folk-songs.'

'I see. Do you sing an English folk-song by the name of *Tamlin* or *Tam Lin*?' I ventured, pushing my luck with inordinate haste, perhaps.

'I do.'

'How many verses?'

'Truthfully, I never counted them. Around fifty-four!'

My heart gave a leap. Bert Lyodd, from whom I had learned my cobbled version, had only twenty-seven verses!

'Could you sing your version for me, eh, what's this you said your name was?'

'I didn't. But it's Jeannie Armstrong.'

'Mine's —'

'No need to tell me, Paddy Tunney, we've heard of you.'

'Who are we?'

'My daddy and my mammie. They're professional folk-singers. They'd love to hear you. Wait till I get my guitar.' Eh! So she was one of them. Pity! A girl like this needed no crutch. We'd see.

She reached me the fiddle-case and got out her six-stringed instrument. When she began to sing, I knew that this was no ordinary folk-singer. She had a beautiful voice, full of soul and sweetness. Maybe the guitar gave her nerve. Certainly she had no need for it. She sang the whole song and followed with *Saro* and *The Little Swallow*. You all know the one I mean. In fact, it's in Bunting's 1840 book. One seldom hears it sung now. Here it is:

THE LITTLE SWALLOW
I would I were a little swallow
I would rise into the air and fly
Away to that inconstant rover
And on his bosom I'd live and die.

But feathered warblers I cannot follow
All pale and pining in woe I lie
Far, far away from the arms of my darling
In love and longing alone to die.

For joy and pleasure we seldom treasure
When out of measure we love anew
But love gets colder when we grow older
Then fades away like the morning dew.

Another day dawned and our squad was giving an open-air concert down town at the Civic Centre. Afterwards, we were to have lunch in one of Mr Sheridan's many restaurants. When I had done my stint, I noticed a lonely and disconsolate Jeannie on the fringe of the crowd.

I approached. She had been busking and an Irish-American

policeman threatened her with arrest if she continued to distract attention from our performance. She had collected two quarters only.

'What about lunch?' I inquired.

'I couldn't afford it', she confessed.

'Be my guest.'

She consented and we broke bread together. Then the chat turned to songs and singing.

'What about *Tamlin*?' I probed.

'I'll put the song on tape for you if you bring along a cassette. You'll have to give me some of your songs, of course.'

'Of course. A fair exchange is no robbery and what you give to a friend is never lost.'

'You won't be going to that old wild pub where your Irish friends are being entertained this evening, Paddy?'

'Most certainly not', I assured her.

'Fine', she said. 'Then daddy will collect you at Mr Downey's this evening at 7.00 p.m.'

I had a great evening with the Armstrongs. They seemed simple, decent folk, much given to black spiritual songs, and lay around on cushions on the floor as they waited patiently for that *Sweet Chariot* which was coming to carry them home. I got on splendidly with them and was presented with an illustrated book of fairytales written by Mrs Armstrong. The coloured drawings were by her good husband. It is one of my cherished possessions.

The edifying tone of their general performance reminded me of the 'convoy' we had given the English contingent back in Harmon House, Georgetown, on the eve of their departure back to England's green and pleasant land. I had missed Jean Richie that night by a whisker. She was leaving as we entered and was gone before I could call her back. Twenty-four years before she and Diane Hamilton had come north to meet me and were told that wherever they found Kitty Gallagher from Middle Dore, I wouldn't be far away.

They duly arrived in Dore and located Kitty, but no hilt nor hair of the rambling boy of pleasure was to be found.

So instead of encountering the blond bombshell of the Appalachians, we had to be content with a shower of hot gospellers from the bible belt who sang spirituals for hours at the loud of their heads.

As singers they were cat-melodeon, but it must be said they were skilled acrobats. There was one little buckin-barrow of a fellow who freely admitted he was eighty-five years old and who could hunker down, thrust his thin, bony arms under his knees and out again at his ankles and then proceed to walk around on the palms of his hands. He was the sponsor for the group.

In time he came my length. 'Kind sir,' he began, 'I am told you are an Irish Catholic. You must have a store of spiritual songs. Would you ever sing one for us?'

'You were told the truth,' I freely admitted, 'and I shall be happy to sing one of these songs for the company. But first let us hear this fine spiritual singer from Scotland. Allison, will you sing one of your most spiritual songs for these good people?' and I winked at Allison McMoreland, a lively little girl in the Scottish contingent who was always singing or dancing.

She gave us a delightful version of *The Cuckoo's Nest* that would have made Rabelais roll with laughter. Like a stone thrown in among a haggard of sparrows, they took flight and scattered in all directions. Bert Lloyd, who was in charge of the Fair England-Bonnie Scotland crew, was tickled to death, and the party got down to the singing of songs that reflected the seamy side of life.

Of course, I must say the Armstrongs were in no way as irritatingly repetitive or blindingly fanatical as the bible-belters, but there was an air of self-righteousness about them that some people found off-putting. I suffered it gladly to get my hands on the complete version of *Tamlin*.

'Why not consult Child or Bronson?' the scholars may ask.

'No need to make such a fuss. After all, there are a number of versions to be found in the ballad volumes edited by those experts.'

And I must agree, but Child or Bronson are not available in the county libraries of Ireland and copies of their collections are rare and very expensive. So far they do not seem to be issued in paperback. *Tamlin*, as it was sung by Jeannie Armstrong, runs to fifty-four two-line verses and takes twenty-nine minutes and thirty seconds to sing. I have only performed it once publicly in Ireland and that was at a *feile na boinne* in Drogheda where my son John sang verse with me. I don't know why, but none of the audience left. In fact, they applauded us heartily. Maybe we misconstrued their reaction. They could have been expressing relief that the ordeal was over. One can never be certain in such instances.

I have since telescoped every two verses together and reset the ballad to the tune of *Liam O'Reilly*. The wedding of an English ballad to an Irish air has been surprisingly successful.

I sang it in the Cornwall-Devon country where I was on a concert tour with the English folk-song clubs. It was a winner all the way and the highlight of many of my performances.

Some of the revisionist breed sneer at this glorious and dramatic ballad and accuse it of being Victorian, but, be it noted, there was much better poetry written in the Victorian era than there has been in this arid and nihilistic age.

Here's the song with all its high poetry and drama:

TAMLIN
Oh! I forbid you maidens all, who wear gold in your
    hair
To come or go by Carter Hall, for young Tamlin is
    there
And those who go by Carter Hall will leave him one,
    I ween

Either their rings, their maidenheads or else their
   mantles green.

La' Margaret sat in her castle hall, sewing a silken seam
She looked from her window high and saw the grass
   growin' green
She let the thread fall to her knee, the needle to her toe
And she's away to Carter Hall as fast as she can go.

But she hadn't plucked a rose and a rose and a rose but
   scarcelt three
When out there started young Tamlin, saying, 'Leave the
   roses be
Why pluck thou the rose, Margaret, and why break thou
   the wand
And why come thou to Carter Hall without my
   command?'

'Oh, Carter Hall, it is my own, my father giaed it me
And I can come to Carter Hall without the leave of thee.'
So he's taken her by the lily-white hand and by the
   grass-green sleeve
And he pulled her down by the butt end of the bush
   and he never once asked her leave.

And when it was done she gazed around to ask that
   young man's name
But she nothing saw and she nothing heard, but all
   them woods grew dim
So, La' Margaret hoisted her green, green skirt a little
   above her knee
And she's gone back to her own father's hall as fast as
   she can gee.

There were four and twenty ladies fair a'playing at the
   ball
Without it goes young La' Margaret, once the fairest of
   them all
There were four and twenty ladies gay, a'playing at the
   chess

Without it goes young La' Margaret, she's as green as
any glass.

Then out there spoke a waiting-maid, she lifted her
hand and smiled,
'I fear our lady has loved too long and now she goes
with child.'
And out there spoke an old, grey knight, lying o'er the
castle wall,
'It's ever alas! young Margaret for you, but we'll be
blamed for all.'

'Oh, hold your tongue, you old, grey knight, an ill death
may ye dee
Father my baby on whom I will, I'll father none on
thee.'
Then out there spoke her father dear and he spoke meek
and mild,
'It's ever alas! my Margaret', he said, 'Methinks thou
goes with child.'

'And if I go with child, father, myself must bear the
blame
There's not a knight in all your throng could bear the
baby's name
The horse that my true love rides on is faster than the
wind
With silver he is shod before, with burning gold
behind.'

Then out there spoke her mother dear and 'Ever alas!'
cried she,
'I know an herb in the merry, green wood that will
scathe thy babe from thee.'
La' Margaret braided her yellow a little above her breast
And she's away to the merry, green wood, without any
rest.

But she hadn't plucked an herb and an herb and an herb
but scarcely one

When out it started young Tamlin saying, 'Leave the
   herbs alone
Why do you pluck that bitter herb, that plant that grows
   so grey
Except to still that pretty little babe that we got in
   our play.'

'Oh! tell, tell me, Tamlin,' she said, 'for sake that died
   on tree
If ever you were to holy chapel and Christindom did see?'
'I'll tell to you, Margaret,' he said, 'the truth, I will not
   lee
That I have been to holy chapel and was christened as
   good as thee.

'But once upon a summer's morn as hunting I did ride
As I rode east and I rode west, soft strains did me abide
There blew a drear and drowsy wind, and sleep upon
   me fell
And the queen of fairie for 'twas she, she took me to
   hersel'.

'And never would I tire, Margaret, in fairie land to
   dwell
For pleasant is the fairie host, but a dreary tale I'll tell
For once in every seven years they pay a tithe to hell
And I being young and full in flesh, I fear 'twill be my
   sel'.

'But tonight it being the Hallowe'en, tomorrow
   Hallowday
So save me, save me if you will. For all I know you may
For at the murk and midnight hour the fairie host do
   ride
And if you will your true love save by the old mill bridge
   you must hide.

'And first will come the black, black steed and then will
   come the brown

But hurry thou to the milk-white steed and pull the
   rider down
For I'll be on the milk-white steed, a gold star in my
   crown
Because I am a mortal knight they gave me that renown.

'And they will change me in your arms into many a shape
   so wold
But hold me fast and fear me not. I'm the father of your
   child.'
'But how will I thee ken, Tamlin, and how will I thee
   know
Among so many unco knights the like I never saw?'

'My left hand will be gloved, Margaret, my right hand
   shall be bare
And cocked up shall my helmet be, no doubt I shall
   be there.'
Cold and stormy blew the wind and dreary was the way
As Margaret in her mantle green, to the old mill bridge
   she did gae.

And at the dead hour of the night she heard their bridles
   ring
And oh, my boys, that pleased her more than any mortal
   thing
And first went by the black, black steed and then went
   by the brown
But hurried she to the milk-white steed and brought the
   rider down.

And thunder rolled across the sky and the stars shone
   bright as day
And the queen of elf she gave a trilling cry, 'Young
   Tamlin's away!'
And the first thing they changed him in her arms was a
   lion and bear so wild
But she held him fast and feared him not; he was the
   father of her child.

And the next thing they changed him all in her arms
    was into an adder and snake
But she held him fast and feared him not; he was one of
    God's own make
And then they changed him in her arms to a red-hot bar
    of iron
But she held him fast and feared him not, and to her he
    did no harm.

And then they changed him in her arms into the burning
    lead
And she flung him into the well water and she flung
    him in with speed
And the last thing they changed him in her arms was
    into a naked man
And she flung her cloak all over him, and cried, 'My
    love, I've won!'

And out then spoke the fairie queen, out of a bush of
    broom,
'She who has gotten young Tamlin has gotten a stately
    groom.'
And out then spoke the fairie queen, out of a bush of
    rye,
'She has gotten the stateliest knight in all my company.'

Out there spoke the fairie queen and an angry queen
    was she,
'Woe betide her ill-starred face and an ill death may she
    doe!
If I had only known, Tamlin, before that we left home
I'd have torn out your heart of flesh and stuck in a heart
    of stone!'

Then out there spoke the fairie queen, with her face as
    red as blood,
'I'd have torn out your two grey eyes and put in two
    eyes of wood.'

'If I had only known, Tamlin,' the elfin queen did say,
'I'd have paid my tithes seven times to hell before I'd let
   you away.'

We left Chicago and headed west to the prairies and the
land of soya beans and corn around Fort Dodge, Iowa.
Hijacking was rife at the time and so the airport security
checks were stricter than usual. At O'Hare Airport, where
we embarked for the prairie land via Des Moines, things
were pretty sticky.

I was fortunate to be frisked by a pretty girl with sparkling
eyes and magnificent undulating curves. As she passed the
metal detector over me it went bleep! bleep! bleep!

'I'm afraid you'll have to empty out your pockets, sir', she
informed me apologetically. I obliged. Medals, coins and a
rosary were piled on the desk before us. She did another run
with her detector but as she approached a vital area in the
region of my belly button her machine bleeped again.

'What ever can be causing it?' she asked me, not a little
perplexed.

'I wish I knew', I told her with absolute conviction and
was as worried as she. Then the truth struck like the shaft of
light that unhorsed Paul on the road to Damascus. The metal
zip on my fly!

'Excuse me, dear,' I began, 'but could the metal zip on my
fly be the cause?'

She flicked back the cloth overlap that concealed the culprit
with a magnificent gold biro and stared hard at the closed zip.
'Hell! shit', she exploded, 'Why the heck didn't you mention
this at the start?' But before I had time to reply she quipped
mischievously, 'You Irishmen with your built-in warning
devices!' Both of us laughed. We appeared to understand
each other. Still, she had had the last laugh. We carried on
to Des Moines Airport. Security was very tight there too. We
were confronted by bulky, boorish male guards whose belts
bristled with guns. Courtesy was a virtue they had obviously never heard of and they hurled vulgar, four-letter

expletives at one another as they hustled us through the barricades.

I was carrying one of Frankie Gavin's fiddles. One of them looked up. His countenance was a cross between that of Don Quixote de la Mancha, with its long, lonely look, and the scar-marked visage of Dirty Dick, an ugly and murderous looking screw-back at the Crumlin Road Academy, Belfast.

He scrutinised our little band. 'Where's the guy with the bleeping fly', he scoffed. The moment of truth had overtaken me. I stepped forward. 'Go ahead, bleeping fly', he growled. There was a titter all the way down that line of troubadours, but I remained poker-faced.

Sonnie McDonagh, my fluting friend from Bunanadden, fared less well. They took him aside and frisked him thoroughly. This was a frequent occurrence on the tour but we never learned why. He was a big man, to be sure, but one less like Fidel Castro or other bearded revolutionaries who strutt about the globe like gobbling turkey cocks it would be hard to find.

We boarded a bus and were driven over trails that were mere dust tracks to the parched little city of Fort Dodge, Iowa, with its fifteen-thousand souls. It is their boast that they are free of racial troubles, but then they have only one black family whose children have gone away.

We were greeted by Canon McAvoy, the parish priest. He is the only Irishman there. He led us to a newly erected platform on the square where a spinsterish-looking schoolmistress coaxed *When Irish Eyes are Smiling* out of a wheezy piano. It put me in mind of Jimmie Cox's racy rendition of that hoary old number:

> When Irish bacon's fryin' and lepin' on the pan
> You can hear the donkeys roarin', comin' down at
>   Hughie's John's.

Canon McAvoy introduced us as worthy ambassadors from the land of saints and scholars, and the multitude assembled there raised their eyes in anticipation of our wing-sprouting and flight away over the prairie. Some of the more daring ladies touched us to ensure that we were not angels of paradise. It was, I assure you, a most gruelling experience.

A certain Doctor Strange was host to Sonnie McDonagh and myself. He was chief of a medical syndicate, a millionaire and owner of a two-hundred acre rosewood forest some fifty miles west of the city. We went out there on an oppressively hot day to inspect the forest. Shorts, sleeveless shirts and sandals were the order of the day. The place was swarming with grass snakes, but they were not venomous. In fact, they were lazy, sleepy creatures that did not move even when we trod upon them. Doctor Strange reckoned that when the timber matured it would be worth a small fortune.

He had good hands and fashioned a metal-strung harp that was the exact replica of the one in Trinity College, Dublin. However, he could not play and neither could any of us.

Although a wealthy man, he did not believe in rearing his family of four with silver spoons in their mouths. Instead, he had them up at 6.00 a.m. every morning to manually pollenate corn out on the prairie. They did this work during university vacation. Doctor Strange loved the art of story-telling and we spent a long summer evening on his veranda, under the protection of mosquito nets, as I retold the story of the 'Tain Bo Cuailgne,' or 'The Cattle Raid of Cooley'. Below us the Des Moine River, poisoned and polluted, slid slowly and silently down the valley while the wood crickets chirped cheerily in the undergrowth. The doctor was entranced by the exploits of Cuchuliann.

'Hell! Why don't you make a film on the life of that guy?' His suggestion had a good deal of merit and I have made it myself on many occasions, but to date even the most fanatical of *gaeilgeoirí* have not attempted to do so.

Maybe some day a hero will emerge with enough skill and traditional expertise to fulfil the task.

21

From Cullybackey to Glenshesk

'We'll have a lock o' gaps and gates to open, I'm afraid, Paddy', John told me as I reversed the car into the mouth of the loanen. 'Ha' ye her locked?'

I replied in the affirmative and followed after my host.

There were, in fact, many gaps and 'slaps' to open and the right-of-way to the old homestead was securely bound by barbed-wire fences, healthy, straight ash saplings and the odd holly bush. We traversed a high platform of turf bank and then descended into water-logged cut-away bog terrain. Although the drainage could be better, it was obvious the task of reclamation had been very thorough indeed. The cut-away bog had been coaxed to grow grass to be sought after by the most fastidious bovine, and this was affirmed by the herd of well-fleshed bullocks that lay on a dry ridge of ground, contentedly chewing their cuds and literally as full as ticks.

However, there was no sign of man or woman stirring within sight or earshot:

> Ill fares the land, to hastening ills a prey
> Where wealth accumulates and men decay.

But who would listen to Goldsmith today in this, the age of the tractor and JCB! It is relevant that a young boy from Belfast on his first visit to the Ulster Folk Museum asked his dad what a spade was.

'I'm not so sure son,' the wise sire replied, 'but I think it's a toothpick used by Finn MacCool in his day.'

'Daddy, he must have had a very big mouth', the boy commented.

'But he was a very big man', the father reassured him.

'Just one more "slap" and we're there', John strove to keep my morale high.

'There's my father's well', he told me, as he stooped down to clear away the undergrowth that hid the stepping stones down to the corbelled well.

'And there, Paddy, was where the wee gate led into the big garden. My mother, I hope she's happy, had an archway over the gate and the wrens built a nest in it. When snow came in the winter time they used to come and shelter in it. When the snow and black frost came you'd get as many as seven of them packed together like sardines in a tin. We grew the year's spuds in that big garden, along with cabbage and leeks. Man dear, you should have seen them leeks! They were as long as your arm.

'Now this was our house. There were three houses in the row altogether. Some yens called it Sydney. I don't know why. None of us were ever in Australia, but ye know the way it is with country folk. They're aye puttin' fancy names on places. Next door to us two ol' lassies lived, Becky and Liza Jane. Becky was always readin' the paper but she never ventured far from home. There used to be great talk in the papers then about Southern Ireland. One day Wullie Scott was in on some errand and says she tay Wullie, "Where's Southern Ireland?" "I'm no too sure," says Wullie, "but I think it's on the other side o' Aughoghil." You know yourself, Paddy, Aughoghil's only down the road from Cullybackey.

'Then there was another ol' boy livin' over here in the other end house. He cut peat and kept a pig. There's the ruin o' the pig-stye still. We'll g'in now tay the ol' homestead.'

To me it was a pilgrimage. Here we were abroad in the Craigs where John Kennedy, County Antrim's finest traditional singer, first saw the light of day. John had spoken lovingly to me about his birthplace many times. I simply had to see it. It put me in mind of my yearly return to the ruins of the old Tunney homestead in the moors of Mollybreen, County Fermanagh, where I sing *The May Morning Dew* to the spirits of the departed. They do everything but applaud.

Sections of the porch have collapsed, but otherwise the house is structurally in fine shape. It was slated with very good slates, possibly what the Gartan man once referred to as 'the Queen's Bangor blue', and there was not a speck of dampness to be seen on the plaster of the internal walls. It was a two-roomed house with a loft over the fireplace, and the beams and boards of the same loft are as sound as the day they came out of the saw-mill.

There was a thick covering of debris and dust on the fire tiles of the hearth stone. John hunkered down and dug it away with a piece of stick. There they were as dry as a bone and as sound as the day they left the kiln. Everywhere the mark of good tradesmanship was evident. What has this plastic and tinsel age done to us at all!

We looked out on the back garden through the space where a back window used to be.

'There's the wee garden where I grew early spuds, scallions, watercress and garlic. Man dear, when I was a wee fella I thought it was the garden of Eden!' he declared with undisguised affection. 'Sure, wasn't it there I was the evenin' in 1952 and my mother was listenin' tay *The Job of Journey Work*. Ye mind the lovely traditional programme Ciaran MacMathúna used to have on the wireless. He had you on singin' *The Lowlands of Holland*. "John, son," she shouted, "come on in here quick. Do ye hear that man? When you can sing like that I'll die satisfied." That was the first time I heard you, Paddy, and I always imagined you to be a big giant of a man.'

'No doubt you were disappointed, John, when we did meet', I joked.

'They say *guid guids* go in small parcels, and then wasn't Cuchuliann a small man!' was John's response.

'With respect to your mother's memory and to please her spirit the least I can do since we are here is to sing her *The*

Lowlands of Holland', I said and then went on to sing the song. John was visibly moved and looked out at his garden of Eden while I was singing the song.

We returned to his home in the picturesque little village of Cullybackey, and there, in the comfort and cosiness of his drawing-room, he sang for me that beautiful and poignant Antrim song, *Lovely Glenshesk*. John's words are different and much more colourful than those in published editions.

LOVELY GLENSHESK
Farewell to you, hills and green valleys and the woods
   that spontaneously spring
Where the feathered tribes all of each species and the
   cuckoos melodious do sing
All this beauty I'm leaving this evening, with sorrow I
   have no disgrace
No wonder it grieves me to leave you and part with you,
   lovely Glenshesk.

I have come to the age of discerning, I was taught for to
   keep the command
And we each gave our own graces freely, but I'm bound
   for a far, distant land
Like the bee I will go gather honey, although I'll wander
   in many's a strange place
And no wonder it grieves me to leave you and part from
   you, lovely Glenshesk.

The Israelites they were in bondage, they murmured at
   their going away
They would rather have held to their burdens and worked
   hard there both night and day
But Moses gave them a bright promise. Alas! they did
   sorely transgress
So no wonder it grieves me to leave you and part with
   you, lovely Glenshesk.

Only for Adam and Eve in the garden, sure we all would
   be happy and free

'Twas the serpent tempted Eve in the garden to eat of
    the forbidden tree
We would never have to work or hard labour, and we
    all would be happy and blessed
So I hope you'll avoid all temptation, when I'm far from
    you, lovely Glenshesk.

Sam Henry says this song was composed by John McCormick
from Greenan, in the parish of Culfeightrim away up at the
head of Glenshesk, one of the renowned nine Glens of Antrim.
Some commentators seek to denounce the poet for parading his
biblical knowledge and refer to this 'Ulsterman's tendency' as
if it were a flaw in his psyche. I reject this view completely.
Indeed, I find the parallel of the emigrating poet and the
Israelies in bondage beautifully drawn as is the simile of
our first parents being banished from the garden of Eden.
The felicity Kennedy manifests in his interpretation of this
song shows us a master craftsman at his brilliant best. For one
listener at least, subtle fusion of the spirit with the smack and
tang of elemental things is a most moving experience indeed.
    John, who like many of us inherited a rich store of songs
from his mother and her constant encouragement when he
went forth to sing the praises of this lovely land, has a
most remarkable traditional style. He can not only split a
phrase in two, but can also cut a word without breaking the
continuity of the line. He can introduce a wailing undertone
in the melody he sings almost akin to the peculiar sob in
Gaelic poetry attributed to Saint Colmcille. I know of no
other traditional singer either in Gaelic or English who can
achieve this effect.
    Listen to his rendition of *Corby Mill*. Here the mood has
changed. It is one of hope, of mirth and of light-heartedness.

THE FLOWER OF CORBY MILL
Come all you tender-hearted chaps, I hope you'll
    lend an ear

And likewise pay attention to these few lines I have
here
It's all in praise of a pretty maid I mean to use my quill
She's the blooming rose of Antrim and the flower of
Corby Mill.

It was on the first of January I was goin' to Butler's Fair
I spied this pretty fair maid, she was combing down her
hair
And as I gazed upon her, my heart with joy did fill
She's the blooming rose of Antrim and the flower of
Corby Mill.

It was all for recreation I went to the fair that day
I didn't mean to tarry long when I crossed McMullan's
Brae
But meeting with some comrade lads when I arrived
there
Oh, kindly they saluted me, 'You're welcome to the
fair.'

We went into Mrs Butler's, where there we did sit
down
The jugs of punch came rumbling in, the toast went
merrily round
The silver, it being plentiful, we drunk with right
good will
And we toasted a glass to the bonnie wee lass, the
flower of Corby Mill.

This fair maid to make mention, I will not name her
name
Her parents might be angry, and I myself get blame
She's a mill-girl to her trade boys, and has the best
of skill
She's the blooming rose of Antrim and the flower of
Corby Mill.

I have travelled all this country o'er and part of Scotland
   too
I've travelled England far and near, believe me friends,
   it's true
I've travelled Ireland o'er and o'er, crossed many a glen
   and hill
But an equal yet I ne'er could get to the flower of Corby
   Mill.

This song was collected by Sam Henry from John Smylie
from Limavallaghan, County Antrim, and is said to be the
work of a rural poet by the name of William Brownlee, a
native of Clough.

Corby Mill was almost certainly situated on the Clough
River and was built in 1789 by Ben Shaw. John tells a story
about the same mill.

'One night Ben Shaw was comin' from rakin' and he
heard the mill goin' like buggary. He knew there were
none of his men workin' here, so he dubbed it to be the
fairies. So he shouts in to them, "Be sure to eat the millar's
bannock." Next mornin' there was a piggin' o' meal on his
doorstep.'

John tells a number of stories about John Bradley, reputed
to be the tallest man in north Antrim. 'He could look down
chimneys, Paddy, nae bother at all. One time he came cyclin'
down to the crossroads where the boys had a pitch-and-toss
school. John came cycling along on this high Raleigh bike
and he looked to be in another world altogether to us boys
on the ground.

'"It must be very col' up there John", shouted a wee wart
of a fella who would get it tight to make five feet even when
he was standin' on his tippy toes.

'"Oh, you don't worry, Wulfie", the big man assured him.
"It's a climate you'll never enjoy!" John had great hands
on him. He could fix dresser doors or make beetles and
he never served an hour to any trade. There was this ol'
lassie up near the Craigs and she sent for him to fix an

ol' press she had. She had the name of bein' very "near", ye know. Didn't keep a very good table, if you know what I mean. When the job was done she set him down to tea. The bread was too hard to mould and there wasn't as much butter as would grease your whangs. But the honey was the smallest portion of all. The man had to put on his specs to see it at all. He looked at the bread, then at the butter and finally he put on the specs to discover it was honey she left him on the plate. "Ma'am, I see you keep a bee", he commented.

'Another night he was comin' from a gamblin' match with a neighbour. The neighbour was wild feared of lightenin'. There came on a bad thunder-storm but it didn't last too long. They took shelter in a carthouse along the roadside, but it had an iron roof on it and with every brattle of thunder the boy aye gee' a lep and let a roar out o' him.

'Then all of a sudden the whole storm was over so they ventured out and headed on home. The thunder was gone, right enough, and so were the black clouds. The stars were glitterin', but there was still an odd flash of what we call here "air-shootin".

'They stood tae wather the horses at John's gap, but the boy was aye scannin' the sky for fear the storm'd come back again. Then there was a great flash o' light in the northern sky.

'"God, oh God! John, did ye see thon splank o' lightenin' up near the plough?"

'"Man dear!" John consoled him. "She be to strike a stone!" John had some great spakes.'

Not only is John Kennedy the best traditional singer in Antrim at the moment, but he is also a good tin-whistle player, a sophisticated fife player and a fine flutist. He has been known to beat a drum on occasions also. In short, he is a troubadour in the full sense of the word.

Before we leave him to head for Gleshesk, let us listen to his version of *Dark Lough Na Garr*, a truly great song.

DARK LOUGH NA GARR

Oh, away ye gay landscape, ye garden of roses
In your land a million of luxuries rove
Restore to me the rocks where the snowflake reposes
If still they are faithful to freedom and love.
Yet Caledonia, beloved are your mountains
As o'er your high summits the elements war
Where the cataracts foam, instead of smooth-flowing
    fountains
I sigh for the valley of dark Lough Na Garr.

It was there my young footsteps in infancy wandered
My cup was my bonnet, my cloak was my plaid
On chieftains long perished my memory pondered
As oftentimes I wandered in pine-covered glade.
I sought not my home until the day's dying glory
Gave merit to the place of the great polar star
For fancy was cheered by traditional story
Disclosed by the natives of dark Lough Na Garr.

The years have rolled on, Lough Na Garr, since I left you
And years must elapse ere I see you again
Though nature of flowers and verdure has bereft you
Yet still are you dearer than Albion's plain.
England, your plains they are tame and domestic
To one who has rambled o'er countries afar
But give to me the craigs that are high and majestic
The steep rounding glories of you, dark Lough Na Garr.

And now we're in lovely Glenshesk, the subject of
McCormick's rare song of the same name. Denis Cassley,
a traditional singer with a beautiful voice and a talent akin
to that of Robert Cinnamond, lived here and had a fine store
of Glen songs. His version of *The Mountain Streams* is different
from the ones sung by Cathal McConnell, and indeed by
myself, but the melody is one that haunts for many moons
and deserves to be more widely known. Here I give the song
as Cassley sang it:

THE MOUNTAIN STREAMS

With my dog and gun through the blooming heather
To seek for pastime I chanced to stray
When a maid I spied, she was tall and slender
Her looks enticed me a while to stay.

Says I, 'My fair maid, I own I love you
Tell me your name and your dwelling also.'
'Excuse my name, and you'll find my dwelling
Near the mountain streams where the moorcocks crow.'

'If you'd consent and go with a rover
My former raking I would leave aside
I'm doomed to love you, so don't prove cruel
But you consent and become my bride.'

'If my parents knew that I loved a rover
They would tie me down in strong iron bands
And in a dungeon they would confine me
Where is no comfort of any kind.'

'Then you'll call round and frequent my parents
And I'll call round and see yours also
I'll stay at home for another season
Near the mountain streams where the moorcocks crow.'

'Then I'll bid adieu to Scotch and valleys
To yon mountain stream and the plains below
And in my arms, love, I will embrace you
Near yon mountain streams where the moorcocks crow.'

'It's hand in hand we will roam together
By yon mountain streams and yon flower grove
Where the linnet changes his notes most pleasant
Near the mountain streams where the moorcocks crow.'

Now to illustrate the endearing style of this forgotten singer
I am giving you Denis Cassley's *Corncrake Among the Whinny
Knowes*. It is a song fired with the poetry of youth and living
things.

THE CORNCRAKE AMONG THE WHINNY KNOWES

The lass that I love best of all is handsome, young
    and fair
With her I spent some happy hours along the banks of
    Ayr
With her I spent some merry hours where scented clover
    grows
And the echo mocks the corncrake among the whinny
    knowes.

We loved each other dearly; disputes we seldom had
As constant as the pendulum, our hearts beat ever glad
We sought for joy and found it where yon wee burnie
    rows
And the echo mocks the corncrake among the whinny
    knowes.

You maidens fair and pleasure's dames drive to the banks
    of Doon
You'll dearly pay your every cent to barbers for perfume
But rural joy is free to all where scented clover grows
And the echo mocks the corncrake among the whinny
    knowes.

Oh, the corncrake is now away, the burn is to the brim
The whinny knowes are clad wi' snaw that tips the
    highest whin
But when cauld winter is away and summer clears the
    sky
We'll welcome back the corncrake, the bird o' rural joy.

It is interesting that Ford, when he published his new and
approved edition of *The Vagabond Songs and Ballads of Scotland*,
and included *The Corncraik* therein, should apologise in a
footnote for mentioning a corncrake – beautifully feathered
and most melodious of birds – in a love song. He issued this
edition in 1904 and evidently never heard of the magnificent
song written by our Cathal Bui MacGiolla Gunna lamenting

the fate of the yellow bittern, whose singing powers were no more melodious than that of the corncrake. Then there was Piaras Beaslai who wrote a most beautiful poem in Gaelic about a *Traonach a mhill mo Shuan* when he was on the run from the Black and Tans. This brings me to the harsh moment of truth when I must declare that the corncrake is a fastly fading species of bird. I know that it is a migratory bird, but if we go on killing it with chemical sprays and continue destroying its breeding grounds with mechanical diggers and the like, there won't be any left to migrate.

When will another Cathal Bui arise to lament its going and press for some real protection for this bird that told us, with the accuracy of the swallows, that summer is coming and the grass is green?

Glossary

aill: *a cliff, big rock*
ailt: *a steep-sided glen or ravine*

B-men: *N.I. special police*
bawn: *a walled or stoned area of land in the front of a large house; a fortification around a house or an enclosure for cattle*
bean an tí: *the woman of the house; hostess*
benweed: *a weed with a yellow flower*
bogged: *stuck*
booragh: *a home-made rope*
bothóg: *a mud or sod cabin*
bowran (bodhran): *a one-sided drum*
brae-face: *hillside*
brashes: *spells of work*
brearded: *newly sprung wheat, oats or barley*
breast-sleaning: *cutting turf horizontally in bogs where the grain of the moss does not suit vertical cutting*
bruach: *a bank of a river or lake*
busking: *singing or playing music for money in a public place without a licence*

cailleach: *a hag or old woman*
caoineadh: *a cry or lament*
car: *a grin or grimace*
cat breac: *Gaelic-speaking proselytiser*
caulkers: *the turned-down endings of horseshoes to give the animal a firm grip*
ceannt: *a temporary stall or counter in local fairs for the sale of second-hand clothes*

ceapair: *a slice of buttered bread*
ceaped: *stopped or obstructed*
céilí: *(n) a dance or party; (v) to make a visit to a neighbour's*
   house
chandering: *scolding*
chullers: *the purple sacks of loose skin around a turkey's throat*
clarendo: *a lightweight maize husk used for animal feeding*
   between the wars
close-spancelled: *tightly tied or bound*
Conor MacNeasa: *an Ulster king in the time of Cuchuliann*
cope-carlied: *capsised*
coped: *turning sods with a spade to form a seed bed or ridge*
crack: *merry-making; lively conversation*
creel: *a wickerwork basket for carrying turf*
creepy stool: *a three-legged stool used by milkers*
crigs: *the sharp ring of hobnail boots on a flagstone or concrete*
   floor
Crom Cruaidh: *a Celtic god or idol*
cruckin: *a little hill*
cuinneog: *a blade of grass*
cut-jack: *a castrated ass*

dam: *a waterhole where flax is steeped*
diabhal: *the devil*
doughty: *tough*
dudeen: *a clay pipe*

fáilte: *welcome*
féar gortach: *hungry grass growing over a mound where a*
   famine victim is buried: induces a gnawing hunger in those who
   tread on it
foscaidh: *shelter*
   seal foscaidh: *a shelter or break erected outside the external door*
   of a house

gae bolga: *the belly spear used by Cuchuliann to disembowel*
   enemies

garner: *to harvest*
gerning: *scolding; fulminating*
gleed: *a tiny spark or glow of a flame*
grá: *love*
greeshagh: *the dying embers and ashes of a fire in which live coals are raked on an open hearth*
greth: *a straw harness for a donkey to protect its back from the straddle-crutch and creel*
gudgel: *the axle of a wheelbarrow*
guid guids: *good goods*

haggard: *a stack-yard*
hames: *the part of a horse's harness which fits around the collar*
hames, to make a: *to make a complete mess of something*
harry pakeries: *fish fry or small minnows*
haughle: *to scuttle or limp along*
headsheaf: *the top sheaf; finishing touch*
holly wattle: *a length of thick holly wood*

in the rere: *at the latter end; at last*

jibble: *to churn with a churn-dash*
join: *to collect money for the purchase of drink*

kilty: *once distilled 'wash' in poteen making*
knowes: *rough hillocks in mountainous terrain*
knuckle a knee: *to kneel*

laghey: *civil*
lea: *a meadow, grassland or pasture not yet tilled or cultivated*
linnet: *a species of singing bird*
loanen: *a lane*
lúb: *to bend, flex*

male: *meal*
meelamurder: *to kick up a shindy; screaming and screetching*
mering: *mere*

mern ditch: *a boundary fence*
moider: *to confuse*
mórtas cine: *pride of race*
mufti: *civilian dress as opposed to uniform*
murk: *dark and dreary*

ostler: *one who cares for a horse*

paltog: *a blow, thump or wallop*
pandy: *a tin mug or vessel*
pavers: *hob-nailed boots*
pedesticle: *a malapropism for pedestal*
pritties: *potatoes*

raparee: *a highway man; a Robin Hood*
rowan: *the mountain ash or its berries*

sally bushes: *willows*
screak: *the first light at dawn*
seanchaí: *a teller of local tales and lore*
shaughran, to go a: *to go astray*
sheeg: *a large stack of corn or hay*
sheugh: *a drain or ditch for the passage of water*
shillelagh: *a stout blackthorn stick*
singlin': *in poteen making, wash once distilled*
skintling: *a faint trace*
sluagh shee: *the fairy host*
slunk: *a quagmire*
sneds: *shapes*
spalpeen: *a farm labourer*
spar: *a piece of thatching on a roof*
spate: *a flood or surge*
spéirbhean: *a beautiful woman; dream girl*
splanks: *sparks*
sprigging: *needlework or embroidery*
stall: *an abbreviation for stallion; a man*
stirabout: *porridge*

stirks: *two-year-old cattle*
stook: *an arrangement of two rows of slanted sheaves of oats,*
   barley or rye capped by head-sheaves to keep the grain dry
straddle-crutch: *a wooden contraption with two pegs mounted on*
   a straw mat to support two loaded creels
swain: *a love-sick fellow*

tarrah: *terror*
tatty-hokers: *potato harvesters*
toe-plates: *steel-tips on toes of hobnails*
tollies: *potatoes*
tram: *leg*
trepan: *figuratively, to break the heart*
trevalley: *a crowd of people*
troth: *truth*
turas: *pilgrimage*
twig: *to come to the realisation*

walter: *to wallow or roll about*
weemin: *women*
wether: *a castrated ram or male sheep*
whangs: *leather laces*
whetstone: *grindstone*
whitehole curraghs: *a series of water holes in a marshland that*
   have the quality of quicksand
whum: *one of four iron rods that secure crates to the body*
   of a cart

yoe: *a ewe*

Index of Songs